Inspiration
for a Woman's Soul:™

OPENING TO
GRATITUDE
& Grace

Published by Inspired Living Publishing, LLC.
P.O. Box 1149, Lakeville, MA 02347

ISBN-13: 978-0-9845006-1-1
ISBN-10: 0984500618

Library of Congress Control Number: 2016911638

www.InspiredLivingPublishing.com
(508) 265-7929

Cover and Layout Design: Rachel Dunham, www.YourBrandTherapy.com

Editor: Bryna René Haynes, www.TheHeartofWriting.com

Printed in the United States.

Dedication

This book is dedicated to ...

Every woman walking the path of self-discovery and healing.

Every woman who has committed to living authentically, even when it isn't the easiest or most popular thing to do.

Every woman who has passed through the fires of transformation, and emerged with the fierce, love-filled heart of a spiritual warrior.

Every woman who chooses to uplift and support other women in sacred community. By encouraging others to shine, you are bringing light into the world.

And also to ...

My family. I am blessed beyond words by your presence in my life. My heart is filled with gratitude for the love, blessings and grace you gift to me each day.

My sacred team and soul sisters. Rachel Dunham, Brand Strategist and creative visionary at www.YourBrandTherapy. com, who, for the last ten years, has been capturing the visions in my heart and bringing them to life; Bryna René Haynes, Chief Editor at Inspired Living Publishing and Founder of www.TheHeartofWriting.com, who has lovingly guided over

180 of our authors through the birthing of their intimate stories; Kim Turcotte, my Web Project Manager at www.KimTurcotte. com, who brings my websites to life; and Nichol Skaggs, my assistant extraordinaire, who keeps things running with ease and grace.

And also to ...

The visionary authors in this book who entrusted me with their sacred soul stories. It is an honor to share this journey with you and birth your stories into the world. Your vulnerability, authenticity, and courage continue to inspire me.

And, finally, to ...

You, reader! May the intimate, vulnerable stories and sacred truths shared on these pages uplift, and empower you on your path, and inspire you to discover the magnificent ways in which gratitude and grace can transform your life for the better.

Praise
FOR *GRATITUDE & GRACE*

"I couldn't put down *Inspiration for a Woman's Soul: Opening to Gratitude & Grace.* I loved this book and I loved meeting all these courageous women. I laughed, I cried, I was deeply moved and profoundly inspired to bring even more grace and gratitude into my life."

> – **Dr. Margaret Paul**, co-creator of Inner Bonding, coauthor of *Do I Have To Give Up Me To Be Loved By You?* and *Healing Your Aloneness*, and author of *Inner Bonding* and *Do I Have To Give Up Me To Be Loved By God?*

"Gratitude is a superpower that, once fully embraced, is truly life changing. In *Inspiration for a Woman's Soul: Opening to Gratitude & Grace*, Linda Joy has compiled a beautiful collection of moving stories from women who have experienced the abundant powers of gratitude and grace, as they share how their lives have been changed. This is an important book that will inspire true transformation."

> – **Kristi Ling**, best-selling author of *Operation Happiness: The 3-Step Plan to Creating a Life of Lasting Joy, Abundant Energy, and Radical Bliss*

"In *Inspiration for a Woman's Soul: Opening to Gratitude & Grace*, once again Linda Joy has brought together a moving and inspiring collection of stories from experts in the fields of health and wellness. This book is a feel-good gem of goodness to read to start the day, close out the night, or uplift you whenever you need it. Highly recommended!"

> – **Amy Leigh Mercree**, best-selling author of *A Little Bit of Chakras, The Spiritual Girl's Guide to Dating*, and *Joyful Living: 101 Ways to Transform Your Spirit and Revitalize Your Life*

"Read this book! You will be inspired. You will be moved. It will change you."

> – **Terri Britt**, former Miss USA & author of *Women Leaders of Love* and *The Enlightened Mom*

"The stories in *Inspiration for a Woman's Soul: Opening to Gratitude & Grace* reveal how being in a state of gratitude causes the frequency and grace of miracles. Every story is a template to help transcend the impossible. It infuses hope in the belief of the secret energy of the mind, body, and spirit!"

– **Cindy Heath**, Kundalini Yoga Teacher and author of *Real Beautiful:*
The Secret Energy of the Mind, Body, & Spirit

"Wow! Linda Joy and Inspired Living Publishing have done it again. I sit here with tears of sadness and gratitude running down my cheeks. The stories in this book are not just beautifully written, but honest, deeply transformational, and inspirational. Each story is followed by a series of reflection questions that encourage the reader to take a look at her own life and to reflect on the impact of each woman's story on her own life. I am so grateful to each of the authors for their contribution, their wisdom and their willingness to share their stories."

– **Dr. Minette Riordan**, best-selling author of *The Artful Marketer: The*
Fundamental Business Guide for Creative Entrepreneurs

"The thirty-eight voices and stories in *Inspiration for a Woman's Soul: Opening to Gratitude & Grace* inspire appreciation of the gifts in our lives, even those that at first appear not to be gifts at all—illness, abuse, divorce, the loss of a job. The questions for reflection after each chapter support readers to mine their own lives for evidence of gratitude and grace and to celebrate their presence in readers' lives. The themes of healing, forgiveness, empowerment and love offer readers relief from their personal suffering and the opportunity for a powerful shift in consciousness."

– **Lisa Tener**, Book coach, Silver Stevie Award Winner,
Mentor/Coach of the Year 2014

"*Inspiration for a Woman's Soul: Opening to Gratitude & Grace* is an incredible gathering of stories by strong and courageous women. Their stories not only opened my heart to a greater sense of gratitude, but deeper self love, self worth and forgiveness by inspiring me to release what may no longer serve me and be fully present with grace. I highly recommend this book to women of all walks of life!"

– **Kim Lachapelle**, best-selling coauthor of *Inspiration for a*
Woman's Soul: Cultivating Joy

"The beautiful stories in *Inspiration for a Woman's Soul: Opening to Gratitude & Grace* are like a soothing balm for the soul. Each of the authors shares a story of a pivotal moment in her life that opened her to experience the presence of grace and gratitude in ways that forever changed her perspective of life. Reading these stories feels like receiving an infusion of grace yourself. They offer a great reminder that gratitude and grace can transform absolutely anything when we allow ourselves to open to their blessings."

> – **Tina van Leuven**, founder of InnerDelight, international best-selling coauthor of *Inspiration for a Woman's Soul: Choosing Happiness* and *Inspiration for a Woman's Soul: Cultivating Joy*, and author of *Money and Miracles: 40 Days to The Perfect Relationship Between Who You Are and What You Make.*

"The beautiful and well written book *Inspiration for a Woman's Soul: Opening to Gratitude & Grace* is a must-have for every woman's bookshelf! Each contributing author teaches the reader how to triumph over obstacles and challenges and how to do it in a graceful and elegant way. They also show how appreciation and being thankful and showing gratitude help us get so much more out of life. These amazing, heartfelt stories helped to not only heal my heart, but to guide my heart to have more gratitude and grace in my life."

> – **Kellie Poulsen-Grill,** happiness expert, best-selling author, founder of the Happy Success Ranch Retreats

"*Inspiration for a Woman's Soul: Opening to Gratitude & Grace* is full of grit and grace. Each uplifting and inspirational story encourages readers to reflect and refuel. The journal prompts at the end of each chapter provides an opportunity for deep discovery, soul searching and renewal. This work of art is a bookshelf blessing."

> – **Lorna J. Brunelle**, best-selling author of *The Buoy Projects: A Story of Breast Cancer, Bucket-Lists, Life Lessons, Facebook and Love* and *Dirty Bombshell: From Thyroid Cancer Back to Fabulous.*

"*Inspiration for a Woman's Soul: Opening to Gratitude & Grace* is an invitation to truth. These powerful stories, one after another, bring home the real magic of inviting gratitude into your life: that of receiving grace. You will be inspired. You will be filled with the ineffable quality of possibility. May you be opened to the fullness of life, as I was, after reading these women's stories."

> – **Laurie Seymour**, Founder The Baca Journey

"The transformational stories in *Inspiration for a Woman's Soul: Opening to Gratitude & Grace* inspire readers to create a satisfying life full of magic and miracles. No matter where you are on your journey, the deeply personal narratives shared in this book will help you open to living from a place of appreciation and will inspire you to begin living the fullest expression of who you are."

— **Shann Vander Leek**, Transformation Goddess, best-selling author, award-winning producer

"*Inspiration for a Woman's Soul: Opening to Gratitude & Grace* is a rare book that will stay with you for a very long time. It genuinely explores the challenges and often life-threatening circumstances each author faced and how they rose above them with the healing power of gratitude and transformative grace. A loving introduction by publisher Linda Joy, heart opening stories, and activities to unburden your heart and be free."

— **Dr. Jo Anne White**, international award-winning, best-selling author, Certified Professional Coach, and Energy Master Teacher

"*Inspiration for a Woman's Soul: Opening to Gratitude & Grace* is a beautiful compilation of heartfelt, vulnerable, and inspiring stories shared by an incredible gathering of women. As each author shared her path to gratitude I felt my heart open to a new level of love and compassion for my own journey and a flow of gratitude touched every area of my life. Within each story I could see parts of myself. I could see my mother, my sister, my friends and the themes that connect us all. A soulful revelation of the power of gratitude!"

— **Lori Andrus**, Shamanic Priestess

"Wow! *Inspiration for a Woman's Soul: Opening to Gratitude & Grace* is a masterfully transformative read. Each story takes you on a journey of self-discovery, healing, growth and release. These pages not only nourished my soul, but inspired me to keep going no matter what dark nights I may face--we all face them. Thank you for crafting this soul-edifying masterpiece that will knit together the hearts and spirits of women around the globe in a poignant and soothing way just as it did for me. This is a must read for every woman."

— **Katie Mazzocco**, founder of www.RevolutionaryProductivityAcademy.com, Small Business Systems Strategist, author of *Revolutionary Productivity: How to Maximize Your Time, Impact, and Income in Your Small Business*

"Gratitude and grace are a potent combination and one is incomplete without the other. Linda Joy understands that on a heart level and brings together other women's hearts in this new book *Inspiration for a Woman's Soul: Opening to Gratitude & Grace* to share their life experiences and deep wisdom of how gratitude and grace touched their lives positively. It's pure joy for the heart to read these courageous and loving women's life stories. The stories inspire, motivate, and most of all give you immense courage. I love this book and all it embodies. Every woman needs this inspiration on her bed stand!"

– **Zeenat Merchant Syal,** Counseling Psychologist, Spiritual Counselor, motivational speaker, naturopath, holistic healer, writer, and founder of PositiveProvocations.com

"In Linda Joy's, *Inspiration for a Woman's Soul: Opening to Gratitude & Grace,* you will connect to women, like you and me, who have bared their souls in order to share how grace and gratitude helped them transform their thinking during life's difficulties. A great reminder for all of us that demonstrates the healing power of grace and gratitude despite the chaotic appearing events of our lives."

– **Lisa Hutchison, LMHC,** #1 international best-selling coauthor, coauthor of two *Chicken Soup for the Soul* books, Intuitive Licensed Psychotherapist, Certified Angel Card Reader

"*Inspiration for a Woman's Soul: Opening to Gratitude & Grace* is a gorgeous book with beautifully written stories that flow from the heart of each author and speak to the soul of the reader. We are reminded that spirit is always nearby, caring for us, teaching us, and lifting us into an understanding that changes the direction of our life, always leading us in the way we are meant to grow."

– **Janet G. Nestor,** author, licensed professional counselor, and Energy Psychologist

"Once again Linda Joy has harnessed the healing power of story with *Inspiration for a Woman's Soul: Opening to Gratitude & Grace*. What a beautiful and soul-igniting collection of wisdom, courage and lessons lived and learned. We can see ourselves reflected in the stories of each of these amazing women, with the prevailing awareness that we are so much more than our circumstances. Read this book, and you'll be more connected than ever to your own capacity to cultivate grace and the magic of gratitude … like medicine for the soul!"

- **Michelle Leath,** founder of liveandeatfearlessly.com

Foreword

Di Riseborough

*T*he practice of gratitude is not new; it is one of deep, innate soul wisdom passed down through the ages, and is the glue that sustains the best of both our society and our personal connections with others.

If gratitude is a state of being that is essential to a good life, why then do we not cultivate and express it on a daily basis? Perhaps the fast pace and multiple distractions of life have made it all too easy for us to forget the importance of gratitude.

The self-help shelves in any bookstore are lined with books on gratitude; images on social media abound with statements like, "An attitude of gratitude," or, "If you want to find happiness, be grateful." These are great on the surface, and when life is going well, it does feel good when we are thankful for our blessings. However, how do you tell someone who has been diagnosed with a life-threatening disease, someone who has been betrayed by a partner, someone who has lost a child, or someone who has lost their job to be grateful in the moment, when the pain they are feeling is overwhelming?

Where are the blessings in our suffering?

In today's world of instant gratification, many are looking for quick fixes to take away the hurt, overwhelm, or confusion. New gurus have emerged, claiming to know "the secret" to help fix your life, but these fixes are often unsustainable. So, what's missing?

A quick fix creates an awareness of something you have to change, and then reveals an action to take to bring about that change. Change that is sustainable involves more than awareness and action; it involves acceptance, love, and risk. You can't run away from your life, no matter how hard you try. It can be scary to face yourself and make choices, but the practice of gratitude provides healing, encourages growth, and enhances your inherent nature.

Gratitude is a high-octave spiritual emotion that opens up our hearts. It is a learned skill, and needs to be cultivated over time and with repeated practice. Interestingly, you cannot be grateful and miserable at the same time. It is impossible to feel fear, worry, and negativity when we engage in gratitude from its truest sense. Gratitude and grace live in the state of love: love for oneself, love of others, love of the journey traveled. It's a daily process that is blessed by time: time to slow down and pay attention, time to honor oneself, time to grieve, time to accept, and time to let go.

When my grandmother was murdered, I did not see the blessing in the situation. I would have liked a "quick fix" to take away my pain—but, like the women whose powerful stories fill this book, I had to come to grips with the emotional turmoil of what had happened. Finding the courage to face my pain and situation opened my heart to a place of gratitude, and ultimately to an experience of divine grace. Standing in the prison, I held the man who had murdered my grandmother in my arms, forgave him, and asked him to forgive himself.

In that moment, I experienced awe, gratitude, and unconditional love. *This* is grace: when you are in harmony with yourself, others, and the power that creates the cosmos, and you are channelling divine love.

Gratitude acknowledges connection—yes, even to those who have hurt us. Perhaps that is the reason why it is central to spiritual traditions worldwide. Every language in the world has a way of saying "thank you." This is because gratitude is an inherent quality that resides within each human being; it crosses all boundaries.

The human spirit is always reaching for the reclamation of its own well-being. The longest relationship we have is with ourselves. Therefore, an important component of your life's experience is to befriend yourself as you are.

To do this, it is necessary to extend appreciation to yourself, to at least the same degree you offer it to others.

Gratitude is more than a tool for self-improvement; it is a way of life. The daily practice of gratitude keeps your heart open, regardless of what comes your way. When your heart is open, grace becomes your state of mind; it acknowledges your adversities, and helps you transcend them.

Each woman in this book was opened to gratitude and grace by paying attention and staying in the present moment. Each woman acknowledged her emotions, her fears, and her situation; each honored her process with loving kindness, tapped into the resilience of her spirit, and remembered that she was infinitely supported by the divine consciousness that resides within her. Each woman surrendered to the process.

When you recognize that gratitude is not simply an emotional response, but also a choice you make, it awakens another way of being in the world, one that nurtures the heart and helps to create a life of meaning and purpose.

Gratitude is the way the heart remembers. It recognizes kindnesses, cherished interactions with others, the compassionate actions of strangers, surprise gifts, and everyday blessings. By remembering, you honor and acknowledge others who have touched and shaped who and what you are.

Gratitude requires you to see how you've been supported and affirmed by other people and the divine—even if, at the time, you might not have felt that support and affirmation. We are constantly benefitting from the skills, creations, and kindnesses of others, from the creation of the telephone which connects us, to those that hold a door open for us, and the nurses who take care of us.

As witnessed in this book, the miracle of gratitude will shift your perception to such an extent that it changes the world you see. Gratitude is like the ocean, majestic and full and grace is the buoy that surrenders to the ebb and flow knowing all is well in the present moment.

As Denis Waitley said, "Happiness is the spiritual experience of living every minute with love, grace and gratitude." Regardless of your life experiences and situation right now, you have the choice to welcome gratitude and grace into your life right now. If you so choose, you won't be sorry.

In gratitude and grace, my friend,

Di Riseborough
Intuitive Life Strategist, #1 best-selling author of
Forgiveness: How To Let Go When It Still Hurts

TABLE OF
Contents

Introduction

Linda Joy, Publisher

*W*hat role does gratitude play in your life?

For me, it's a state of being. When I'm operating from a place of gratitude, I can do my best work, clearly hear the guidance of my heart, and step forward as my most authentic self. But it wasn't always this way.

Twenty-six years ago, I was a single mother on welfare. My future looked darker than a thunderstorm. Every day, I struggled to meet my basic needs and those of my young daughter. Yet, there was a small, deeply-connected part of me that *knew* there was something better out there for me.

One day, I picked up a book in the self-help section of the bookstore. I wish I could remember the name of that book, because it changed my life—but all I remember now are the simple instructions it gave: "Each morning, write down five things for which you are grateful."

Five things? I had to find *five things* to feel grateful for every single day? It was hard for me to think of a single one!

But something inside me pushed me to try. Every day, I found five things for which I could feel gratitude. Sometimes it was only the feeling of the wind on my face, or the fact that my rattletrap car was still on the road. Other times, it was the kindness of a stranger, or the unconditional love I received from my little girl.

With practice, it grew easier and easier to shift my attention from fear and longing for what I *didn't* have in my life to gratitude for what I *did* have. Within three months, I was overflowing with things to feel grateful for. I added an evening gratitude practice, so that I could carry that feeling of love and trust with me into sleep. Each night, I would lie in bed with my eyes closed, and list all of my blessings until sleep carried me away.

In those moments, when I let my negative thoughts slide away and let the essence of gratitude fill my heart, I had my first true experience of *grace*.

As I shifted within, my outer world started to change, too. New opportunities came my way. I was able to get off welfare. A few years later, I launched my first business, and since then have followed the calling of my soul: to inspire women to step into their greatness and create their most authentic lives.

Today, holding the essence of gratitude in my heart is what keeps me connected to my divine Source, and keeps the energy of grace present in my life. In any given moment, if I'm feeling frustrated or disconnected, I know it's because I'm not operating from a place of gratitude.

To date, I've worked with over 180 authors and released five collaborative books—as well as my flagship solo author book, *Being Love: How Loving Yourself Creates Ripples of Transformation in Your Relationships and the World* by Dr. Debra Reble—through my publishing imprint, Inspired Living Publishing, and I've started to notice a common thread. In each of these inspiring books, regardless of the individual subject matter, gratitude is a central theme.

When we begin to live from a place of gratitude, we can begin to create real change in our lives. When we embrace gratitude in every moment, even when our current circumstances reflect something vastly different than what we desire, we invite grace into our lives.

What is grace? To me, it's that place of peace and serenity where I feel in complete alignment with All That Is. To the inspiring women who contributed their stories to this book, it means many things: trusting the universe, taking a leap of faith, or receiving the solution to a seemingly unsolvable problem. However, as you'll experience in every one of these powerful stories, transformative moments of grace rarely happen unless the woman opens herself, through gratitude, to receive them.

Gratitude is the foundation that helps us discover grace—but grace is fluid. We, as humans, are dancing with grace, weaving in and out of it from moment to moment, following the thread of our personal divine connection. At times, we stumble; at other times, we step off the path altogether. But the more we embrace gratitude, remember our truth, and stay in that positive energy field, the more consistently we can allow grace to embrace us.

Melody Beattie wrote, "Gratitude unlocks the fullness of life. It turns what we have into enough, and more. It turns denial into acceptance, chaos to order, confusion to clarity. It can turn a meal into a feast, a house into a home, a stranger into a friend." No matter what your current situation looks like, it is possible to feel gratitude. You only need to choose it—just as I did, twenty-six years ago.

It is my hope that the heartfelt, lovingly-offered stories in this book will open you to the power of gratitude in your own life, and set you spinning in a new, more deliberate dance with grace.

From the bottom of my heart, I offer my gratitude for you, reader. Thank you for inviting this book into your hands, and into your heart. May it bless you as deeply as its creation has blessed me.

With Love,

Linda Joy

CHAPTER
One

Grace is ...
Choosing Wholeness

Loving Myself Whole

Dr. Debra L. Reble

On a typically gray winter day in Cleveland, I sat on the edge of the examining table in my oncologist's office, gazing out the window and trying to soothe the terror that was rising within me.

Just yesterday, I had been planning our spring vacation to New York City, driving my daughter to middle school, and sending care packages to my son at college. Just last week, I had committed to finishing my first book. Just six years ago, I'd met the love of my life, and married him in a romantic ceremony in Florence, Italy.

And just last month, I'd gone in for a routine mammogram ...

Now, here I was, with the crackly tissue paper gown grazing my breasts, jolted into a reality I could never have imagined.

As I sat there, a million thoughts ricocheted through my head at once. *Who will take care of my children? What if I lose my breasts? What if I die?* It struck me as ironic that I had actually been considering a breast reduction in the next year.

My doctor walked into the room and, with little small talk, shared the results of my suspicious mammogram: a small area of calcification on my right breast.

I took a breath. No, I could never have imagined this, but it was real.

After a series of follow-up mammograms, an ultrasound, and a needle biopsy, I was diagnosed with invasive ductal breast cancer, and a lumpectomy was scheduled.

Having weathered my challenging childhood, two divorces, single parenting, and the loss of my mother at eight years old, I had learned to bounce back quickly from even the most devastating circumstances.

However, this information rocked my world more than anything I had ever experienced before because of my underlying fear: that my children would lose me like I lost my own mother.

Like resuscitation paddles that jump-start the human heart back to life, the sheer vulnerability I felt after that diagnosis shocked me out of my complacency with my health. My world turned topsy-turvy overnight. Yet, whenever I turned inward, I knew that a path of transformation was being laid for me, and I trusted that, as long as I remained connected to divine grace, everything would be fine.

I was being given a wake-up call to open my heart. It was time to release the energy blocks around my heart center, and the deep-seated emotional patterns—especially self-consciousness, worthlessness, and shame—that had created them.

Aware that my self-healing required inspired action, I set a clear intention for wellness and surrounded myself with what was to be my energetic support team—those who loved me without judging, enabling, or interfering with my choices, whether or not they agreed with the healing path I had chosen.

Realizing that I was accountable for the flow of energy between my mind, body, and spirit, I quickly shifted from reaction to responsibility. It took focused awareness to capture the negative thoughts, feelings, and patterns I engaged in every day and consciously replace them with positive, supportive, and loving ones—but, bit by bit, I began to do so.

When my head asked, "Who will take care of my children if something happens to me?" my heart would answer, "Your children have a loving support system around them." When my head asked, "How will I tell my children?" my heart reassured me, "You will know the timing and they will be there to support you." And when my head asked, "What if I lose my breasts?" my heart answered, "You are a beautiful feminine energy, with or without your breasts." I also reinforced to myself, "This is an opportunity for your transformation. You are strong enough to handle this. You are a well being."

I tossed out old mindsets, beliefs, and attachments to anyone or anything that no longer spiritually served me. The more I connected to my spirit through my heart, the more my choices became clear and inspired by self-love. At times I felt like a tuning fork that had been struck; as I sang out my new tone, I also set in motion a higher vibrational energy to bring about a miracle of healing.

I had the power within me to invite miracles. Realizing this unleashed a force of love upon the dis-ease trying to take up residence in my body. With this intention, I meditated every day, and connected with the highest vibrational source for healing: love. Harnessing the energy of love through my heart like the light streams in the movie *Ghostbusters*, I directed it to surround every cell in my breast tissue and throughout my body with the intention of dissolving energy blocks and promoting healing.

Several weeks before the lumpectomy, I legally changed my last name, which was my maiden name, to my married name, a change that I believed would energetically separate me from my past and validate my core being rather than my identity structure.

A week before the surgery I traveled with my husband and daughter to New York City to relax and have fun. Near the end of our trip, we visited the Metropolitan Museum of Art, where we went our separate ways. Doug and Alex went to explore the Impressionists exhibit, while I was drawn to the sculpture exhibit with its view of Central Park. While sitting quietly on a bench in the garden, I was overcome with deep sense of gratitude for my life. As I opened my heart in the expansive space of this love, I sensed a shift in my entire being, affirming my connection to divine grace and the sacred truth that everything was part of a divinely-orchestrated plan.

I eventually rejoined my husband and daughter, and we left the museum to walk in Central Park. While there, I continued to experience the flow of grace. It was as if everything before this moment had disintegrated. In my trancelike state, I reached into my pocket for my new leather gloves and realized I had lost one.

I retraced my steps back to the bench in the sculpture exhibit, but never found my glove. I wasn't surprised. I knew that it had disappeared along with my breast cancer.

The day after we returned from New York, I had the lumpectomy. I went into the surgery knowing that I had made a series of intentions and discerning choices that had invited miracles of love and healing. My intention for wellness had already manifested.

The biopsy results were negative for breast cancer. I'd known they would be, but they were completely unexpected by my doctor, who insisted that I schedule radiation and chemotherapy treatments anyway.

Feeling like I had been jerked backwards into a past reality, I let the nurse lead me down the hall to schedule the treatments.

A few hours later, when I was able to step outside of the situation and see it in a different light, I gave myself permission to follow my heart. Trusting myself implicitly, I called and canceled the radiation and chemotherapy, invited a new holistic medical partner into my healing process, and continued to pursue my personal path of wellness.

Today, when I participate in a walk for breast cancer, I walk across the finish line as a "thriver" rather than a "survivor." The distinction for me is crystal clear. Reinforcing that I am a survivor would keep me energetically tied to my past physical experience, causing my cells to vibrate at a lower frequency—but as a thriver, I sustain a higher frequency of love energy and affirm that I have energetically broken with the past.

Ultimately, my healing experience was a miraculous manifestation of the transformative power of love. I am grateful for my experience with breast cancer because it inspired me to walk in the flow of grace, and trust that I am spiritually prepared to handle anything that comes my way, even an unexpected illness.

Almost ten years after being diagnosed with breast cancer, I am still loving myself whole. I am reminded daily of our spiritual ability to make discriminating choices that dramatically alter our life paths, open us to gratitude and grace, and manifest realities beyond anything we ever thought possible.

When was the last time you were able to let go and trust?

_____

_____

_____

_____

Debra found comfort by letting her heart answer the questions in her head. Where in your life can you listen more deeply to your heart?

_____

_____

_____

_____

Debra identifies herself as a "thriver" rather than a "survivor." Where in your own life can you shift the labels you place on your experiences in order to harness their most positive aspects?

_____

_____

_____

_____

11

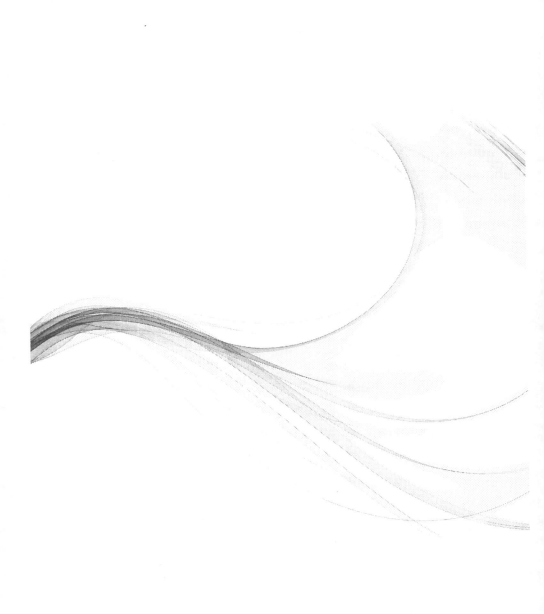

My Beautiful Body

Diana Beaulieu

I felt like my life as a woman was over before it began. I was fourteen years old, standing naked in front of the mirror. Reflected was a budding woman's body, with ripening breasts and dimpled thighs. I was barely breathing. The silence in the house mirrored my voiceless shock.

Last time I'd really looked at myself I had been in a child's body. What had happened? Where had I been all this time while this disastrous change was occurring? Try as I might, I couldn't associate myself with this new body. It looked hideous to me. I'd rather the earth swallow me up than be seen naked by anyone. My child's body was gone forever. I felt only shame, and a vague feeling of guilt; I must have done something wrong for things to be this way.

Shame accompanied me through life like a lead weight. I was tainted. A freak. My hips, my buttocks, my thighs … all felt like a dreadful landscape of *wrongness*. High school and university were a solitary prison sentence. I learned to hide my shame beneath a façade of intellectual achievement, while loneliness clawed into my soul, hardening my heart.

The years passed, and healing came on many levels for me. I discovered my intuitive gifts, moved to a magical Mediterranean island, and built a thriving practice helping others to heal and find happier lives. I had a beautiful daughter with a wonderful man—but when, after years of soul-searching, we found ourselves unable to sustain a satisfying partnership, we decided that the best way to stay united for our daughter was as loving friends.

However idyllic many aspects of my life were, I knew there was a crucial missing piece for me as a woman. I couldn't create a lasting love relationship with a man. I couldn't figure out how to make peace with my body. I couldn't feel my beauty. My shame was deep, unreachable, immovable, and seemingly all-powerful. Why could I not be free to love and be loved?

I begged life for answers, for the magic blade that would cut away my shame and self-loathing.

Nothing could have prepared me for just how hard it would be to get those answers. They came in the form of memories that unleashed themselves into my consciousness without warning. For almost a year, I was laid out in bed for several days a month, seeing, hearing, feeling, shaking, and crying, as my body spewed out its hidden secrets of violent abuse.

My journal entries from this time began like this:

> *"You are evil," he said. "That's why I am doing this to you. And I will kill you if you tell anyone what we did." Shock, fear, and disgust coursed through me. I truly believed I was going to die.*
>
> *My eleven-year-old self could not think of anything evil that she had done. She realized it must be her— her body—that was bad. She swallowed the memory, the one that was too dangerous to hold. She swallowed the truth that she was evil until it was deep inside her body.*

I began to dread the signs of new memory recalls. It was like being dragged down a well, feet first, into a darkness I didn't want to face. Javier, my daughter's father, often held and caressed me as I literally shook these memories out of my body.

Then, finally, the deepest memory came through. In the memory, I was being raped by a family friend.

"It's our secret," he whispered. "Remember, I love you. This is how I show my love."

My seven-year-old self decided to leave. She did not want to be here on Earth in a body. I watched her shoot up into the stars, far away from the pain and fear. She flew up out of reach. She took the memory of everything that had happened with her. She took my innocence and trust with her.

Reliving this final memory took incredible strength. I experienced the physical torture that my seven-year-old self had been unable to process. I was at the end of my strength. Was I going to be haunted by these memories forever?

No. I was going to heal them.

I needed to call back the lost and wounded children who had left me. They held the key to my innocence and joy, but they were caged deep within shadow or were flying high above in the stars. How could they return safely to a body that had always been judged, hated, and denigrated? I could only see one way.

I needed to make my body a place of love.

I began with a daily practice. I placed my hands on every part of my body, one by one. "Thank you," I whispered to each part. To my thighs, my calves, my breasts, my feet, my sex. "Thank you for everything you do for me."

At first, it felt almost impossible to feel gratitude. My "thank you" sounded hollow and false after so many years of self-denigration. But I continued. Gratitude became my daily practice. I would not give up. I gave thanks for my body in front of the mirror each day until I began to see beauty.

Then, one day, I truly let myself feel the incredible miracle of my physical body. Tears coursed down my face as I surrendered to my body in humble thanks. My gratitude had finally become stronger than my shame. I felt my little girls return home where they belonged. I could literally feel their energy entering my legs and hips, grounding me to Earth. I felt that my body truly was a temple for my soul, and I began to love my physical being for the first time ever.

As my little girls returned to my physical being, I felt their pain, loneliness, fear, rage, grief, and shame. I promised that I would care for them and create a safe space for them. My children needed a mother—but could I possibly provide enough love from within me?

As though in response, I felt a huge, empowering presence flood through me and envelop me in warmth and comfort. The Divine Mother whispered, "I am with you now. You can let go of the past."

I felt pure light flood my body as my wounded parts and I surrendered, together, to the purest love imaginable. As tears streamed down my face, I let unconditional love and divine presence enter into all the parts of me that had spent so long in shadow. It was finally safe to experience the grace of being loved unconditionally.

I enjoyed simple experiences in a whole new way. Walking, dancing, basking in sunlight. Weight melted off my body as I shed my old protective layers. It was safe, now, to be beautiful. Gratitude for my body and the grace of self-love were taking me on an upward-spiral dance.

One day, I said "thank you" for my whole experience: for the abuses that had forced me out of my body, and for the gratitude that had invited my soul back in. I even thanked those men who had abused me. They had stained their souls to provide me with a powerful healing and learning experience.

I reached into my soul's wisdom and saw that my entire life was a gift. There was a higher purpose for this journey. I had chosen to experience and heal these terrible abuses so that I could inspire others to recover their beauty, sacredness, and power. There are countless women on Earth who need to heal. I can now help them.

"Thank you, thank you! Thank you for my beautiful body. Thank you, thank you. *Ah-oh!*" My song rang through the air as I danced in front of the mirror, celebrating my forty-one-year-old self as the immensity of the gift of living in my body overwhelmed me again.

Reflection

Where in your life do you carry shame or guilt? How do these feelings affect your daily experience?

_____

_____

_____

_____

Diana found healing in the experience of gratitude and forgiveness— even for those who had abused her. How would it feel for you to forgive someone who has done you a great wrong?

_____

_____

_____

_____

How do you feel about your body? What would it feel like to be grateful for your body as the temple of your soul?

_____

17

_____

_____

_____

Opening to Miracles

Dr. Bonnie Nussbaum, PhD

*T*ravel was typically joyful for me, but not this time. I was flying to Hilton Head Island for a conference on holistic care which I had loved attending in the past. Nonetheless, I felt heavily distracted by the recent unpleasant news that I had a mass on my ovary that would require surgery when I returned. I felt tired, defeated, and irritable.

To top it all off, I had all kinds of difficulties getting to the hotel. I was late getting to the conference, and the talk I *most* wanted to hear was closed because the room was full.

I was really frustrated that I would miss the talk, but decided to try "going with the flow," which is typically not my style. I wandered into another room, where a large crowd was waiting to hear Dr. Lewis Mehl-Medrona speak about Native American healing practices. It was already ten minutes past the time he was supposed to begin—and that irritated me too, even though I'd just arrived. I watched the door, looking for a presenter type to walk in (maybe in a suit, with a professorial air and carrying books) but the slight, unassuming man who took the stage garnered very little attention until he began to speak.

"My guides are telling me to offer a healing on the beach tonight," he explained. "Is anyone interested?"

Many of us were.

"Wonderful. Well, although I am here on Hilton Head, my luggage has vacationed elsewhere. I am without my drums, sacred tobacco, and fire-striking tools."

"I have a drum," someone said from the audience.

"And I have tobacco," someone else added.

By the time everyone was done offering, all the necessary items had been accounted for.

For the rest of the day, I caught myself thinking about the healing that was coming that evening. I'm not sure I heard much of what the other speakers said (although I have the notes to prove I was there and heard their words, at least for the amount of time it took to commit them to my notebook).

An hour before dusk, I left the hotel, made my way through the pool area, and went down the steps to the beach. I felt an unpleasant, anxious anticipation in my chest and stomach as two voices within me battled over whether "healing on the beach" was even a real thing, a possibility. I wanted to let myself be excited, but my internal protective naysayer, present since childhood, waged a hearty battle to suppress any hopefulness. Aiming to soothe my agitation, I decided to go sit near the labyrinth and watch other people walking and meditating.

I knew from past years of attending this conference that a woman came out to the beach every morning when the tide had receded to carve a labyrinth in the sand with a stick. She worked diligently, knowing that every evening, when the tide came in, her creation would be washed away. Remembering her words about the temporary nature of Earthly things, I felt a twinge of panic, because the mass on my ovary had the potential to make my visit here on Earth even shorter. I had two small children, and a husband who stayed home to care for them. I was the primary breadwinner. Without me, their lives would be drastically different.

I vigorously shook my head to clear out those unwanted thoughts.

Now, to my right, I could see Dr. Mehl-Medrona sitting in prayer near the fire he'd built before sundown. I was intrigued and mildly impressed with his ability to be still. I had always been very distractible and hyperkinetic, often getting in trouble as a kid because I couldn't sit still. Even now, as an adult, stillness was not in my skill set. Generally, if my foot wasn't bouncing, I was picking at my fingernails or fidgeting. Dr. Mehl-Medrona, focused and motionless, captured my attention, and I felt a surge of appreciation that he was willing to share his healing gifts with us.

People were beginning to gather, but I resisted the urge to walk over to the fire. The part of me that had been disappointed by people in the past wanted to stay on the bench, tending her tiny flicker of hope. She did not want to walk into the circle and have that hope extinguished.

Finally, I made myself get up and join the crowd around the fire. Dr. Mehl-Medrona rose from his prayer, and motioned for us all to be seated. I hung toward the back of the crowd, almost as if I didn't want to be seen—but when he asked, "Who has the intention for personal healing tonight?" my hand shot up, along with about a half dozen others. I felt a rush of relief that mine hadn't been the only hand raised.

The doctor shared some stories of healing from his tribe's history, and knelt to place some tobacco into the fire. Then he called forward a man near the front of the crowd who had raised his hand. Those in the crowd who had brought drums began to play them. The drumming made me feel anxious, because I couldn't hear the words the doctor was whispering to the man in front of him. I could see that he had a seashell filled with smoking herbs; he was wafting the smoke over the man's body, using a white feather as a fan. When he had finished, he set the shell and feather down and warmly hugged the man.

As he called forth each person for healing, I felt a mounting anxiety in my chest. I prayed I wouldn't be dead last to be called forward, and fought against a resurgence of the desire to hide that I'd often felt as a child in school. After getting in trouble so often for being overactive, I still believed on some level that it wasn't safe to be visible.

I was called forward second to last. As I stood and approached the fire, my legs were so wobbly that I was afraid they wouldn't hold me up. People offered me their hands in support as I picked my way through the crowd. I kept my eyes down for as long as I could, ostensibly to watch where I was stepping, but really because I was afraid to make eye contact with Dr. Mehl-Medrona.

When we came face to face, I raised my gaze to look into his very kind eyes. He began smudging around me, murmuring under his breath. He motioned for me to turn around, then smudged some more. When he was finished, he set down his tools, hugged me, and whispered in my ear, "The angels are very fond of you. Much is planned for you." I stared at him in confusion, but he just smiled, and turned toward the last person to be served.

I spent the remainder of the conference mulling over his words, trying to figure out how they fit into my life. I owned an outpatient mental health clinic, so I already served others, but I often had the feeling that I was supposed to be doing something different—something *more*.

Upon my return from the conference, I made another appointment with my gynecologist and asked him to reassess the mass. I told him, "I know you'll think I'm nuts, but we did a healing on the beach and I want to know if there is any change." He smiled that benevolent smile reserved for those perceived as crazy, but he did another ultrasound, and looked quite surprised when he informed me that the mass was several centimeters smaller than it had been two weeks ago. I just smiled, basking in my tremendous gratitude for the healing energy that had been shared.

Eventually, I did have surgery to remove the mass due to other complications, but I still believe the shrinkage of the mass was a direct result of the healing on the beach.

In the many years since then, my life has transformed in amazing ways, all of which have involved large and small leaps of faith, and all of which were possible as a direct result of the grace that happened on the beach. I've sold my practice, started a holistic coaching business, sold my home, left a very unhappy marriage, purchased a small "Mom-n-Pop" motel which I'm rehabbing into a retreat center, and adopted a nine-year-old black Lab who is my companion in healing.

Each change in my life has been preceded by intense fear and worry—right up until I returned to the faith that was sparked during that beautiful ceremony on the beach.

I feel like I've come full circle in many ways. My motel has Native American features, including a wabeno, a longhouse, and a sweat lodge. I feel a special affinity for the wabeno, a dome-shaped structure that feels very womb-like to me when I'm sitting within its protective walls; it is a place I come to practice gratitude. When I strike a fire in the wabeno, which sits on the site of centuries of sacred fires, I'm reminded of one particular fire on a beach, where dozens of strangers and a slight, unassuming Native American man taught me about opening myself to miracles.

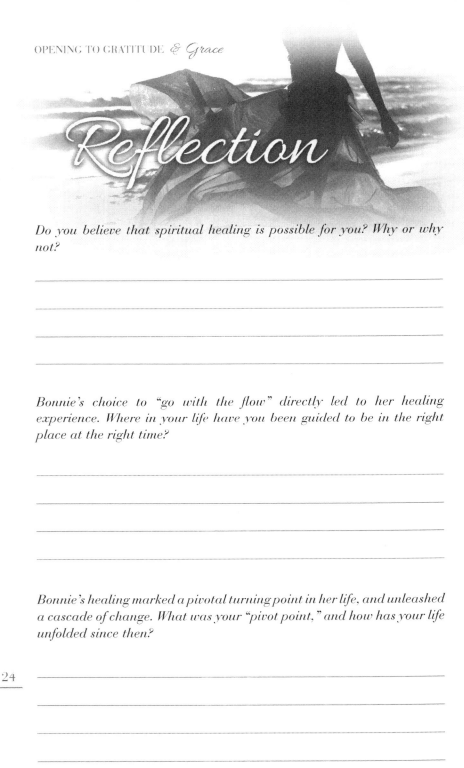

Reflection

Do you believe that spiritual healing is possible for you? Why or why not?

_____

_____

_____

_____

Bonnie's choice to "go with the flow" directly led to her healing experience. Where in your life have you been guided to be in the right place at the right time?

_____

_____

_____

_____

Bonnie's healing marked a pivotal turning point in her life, and unleashed a cascade of change. What was your "pivot point," and how has your life unfolded since then?

_____

_____

_____

_____

Finding the Balance

Felicia D'Haiti

I had what seemed like a million papers to write during my senior year in college, all due the same day. Why hadn't I started them earlier? I never imagined I could be so busy, nor have so much to do. Not having a computer, I handwrote drafts and then typed the final versions on a typewriter. For three days I wrote whenever I wasn't in class, and at long last I submitted my term papers. Suddenly, I realized that I was hungry. Why was I so hungry? Oh, probably because I hadn't eaten anything in the last three days.

I never thought much about that week until recently. Life continued. It was normal for me to do whatever was necessary to get things done. I felt determined and happy, and somehow always completed my long to-do list. People often remarked that they didn't understand how I did it all. This sentiment continued after graduation and throughout the next twenty years as I married, had four children, and managed the family activities—all while juggling a full-time teaching job, a second business, and all the responsibilities that came with both. To me, it was no big deal. I always got everything done. Life continued to move along—until it unexpectedly came to a screeching halt last August.

That summer was even busier than usual with work, summer programs, conference travel, and my twentieth wedding anniversary trip to Hawaii with my husband. When we returned, there wasn't much time to fit in my annual medical checkup. I nearly canceled my appointment after rescheduling it several times, but finally went to see my doctor just before the start of my school's professional development week.

As soon as I arrived, my doctor asked if I had fasted for my blood test. I hadn't. She began to explain that she wanted me to fast after midnight, and then come in the next morning to take my test. After looking at my records, however, she changed her instructions. She actually said that she didn't trust that I would come back the next day, because I had failed to do so the year before. She was correct: her office was out of my way, and I didn't have time to go there just for a blood test. She also wanted me to take other screening tests that I had avoided because I felt fine, and because I didn't want to make time.

Why is she trying to make me take tests that are recommended for people older than me? I wondered. *I'm only forty-six, and I feel totally healthy!*

Because the doctor was so insistent, I took all of the recommended screening tests—then quickly forgot about them and went back to gearing up for the new school year.

Near the end of the following week, I received a phone call from one of the nurses. She said the doctor wanted me to have a colonoscopy. My first thought was, *Yuck! Another test?* The school year had just started. Once the students begin school, teachers can't take leave for the first two weeks. So when the nurse called, I told her I would have to push the appointment back until September. She insisted that I come in before that.

I wondered what was wrong with the doctor and her nurse. They were interrupting my well-planned schedule. I didn't want to take time off from work. I didn't want to go through the procedure. I felt fine, and I was *busy.* All of my thoughts focused on the total inconvenience of the situation.

I was able to get a one-week postponement out of them, but that was it. I had my colonoscopy on August 31, still lamenting the annoyance of it all. I was missing work, and the horrible drink I'd had to consume before the procedure had interfered with my family's end-of-summer trip.

When I woke up from the procedure, the doctor asked if she could bring in my husband. Then she said something that came as a complete shock. I felt as if I was suddenly separated from my body, not quite hearing or comprehending what she was saying. She continued to talk as I absorbed—and then deflected—every word she said. Sensing that I wasn't fully believing her, she pulled out pictures to illustrate what she'd been trying to tell me: that I had cancer in my colon and would need surgery.

The next day, I went back to work, back to the busyness. Yet for the first time in a long time, I felt like I wasn't in control of my life.

Within two weeks, I went to the hospital for the surgery to remove part of my colon. I still believed that this was just a little bump in the road, and that I'd be back to work in no time—but that didn't go as planned either. Prior to leaving the hospital, the surgeon reviewed my post-surgery test results, and told me I would need to see an oncologist, because the cancer had spread outside of my colon.

A few weeks after my surgery, just before I began chemotherapy, my primary-care doctor—the one who'd ordered all those tests I didn't want to take—called to check on me. Oddly enough, it was a pleasant surprise. During our conversation, I thanked her for insisting that I follow through with all of the tests. She was quiet for a moment, and then said in quite a gentle and loving voice, "No, honey. It wasn't me. It was the angels. And they are still looking after you."

At that moment, I was suddenly pulled out of my daze. I could feel my body again, and was aware that I was healing—that I was *meant* to heal.

It was after that conversation that the memory of my "forgetting" to eat for three days in college popped back into my head. Though I practiced yoga, meditation, and other forms of energy work, and also taught others how to incorporate these practices into their lives, was I *really* practicing the essence of what I taught? Did I take the time to care for myself first? Or did I take care of everyone and everything else first, and take care of myself only if I had extra energy?

Throughout much of the next several months, I continued to work when I could, to manage events and projects with the children, and to get things done. It was difficult for me to ask for and accept assistance. I wanted to continue to do everything for everyone—but my body would not cooperate. I needed assistance to get out of bed, to walk, to cook dinner, and to do other everyday things I took for granted. I had to open myself up to receive help.

As I reflected on the conversation with my doctor, I began to accept that I am not a one-woman army. Others are present to support and take care of me, even when I don't take care of myself. The process of accepting assistance from others has been the most difficult part of my journey, but now I see the necessity for balance between giving and receiving. Each time I've felt like I was alone, or it was too much trouble to ask for help, I've received a text, e-mail, or call from a friend checking on me. "What do you need?" they ask. "What can I do for you?" It took a few months for me to admit that I could use help with tasks like family meals. I started forcing myself to make lists of what I might need, so that if someone asked I would have a meaningful response. If I didn't have the list, I would just say that I didn't need anything—and that habit wasn't helping anyone.

It also took me a few months to realize that going to work was slowing my healing. So, after being reminded (and jokingly threatened) numerous times by colleagues to "just stay home," I finally did. The last two months of my treatment were dedicated to healing and learning to practice self-care.

I had my final chemo treatment just days before I submitted my revisions of this story. I'm so grateful for all that this journey has taught me. Before, I was accustomed to giving and going non-stop; now, I have learned to receive care from others, and allow the grace of their generosity to light up my life.

How do you practice self-care in your daily life?

_____

_____

_____

_____

What can you do daily to create a balance between giving and receiving?

_____

_____

_____

_____

What would it look like if you asked for help and support whenever you needed it?

_____

_____

_____

_____

A Choice of Grace

Dr. Kimberly McGeorge, ND, CNH

*S*ometimes, it's the little things that get you.

Wrangling four preteen and teenage daughters is a bit like herding cats, but after a few "I forgots" and "hold its" we were on the road, and looking forward to spending a day by the lake.

I might have been a little selfish in organizing this outing. I'd been working long hours, traveling, and bringing work home with me. A day with the girls, without distractions: that was all I wanted.

As we approached the booth to enter the lake area, a big sign welcomed us: "The Park is Closed Until Further Notice."

Not a big deal, you'd think, but it really crushed me. It was the last drop that made my bucket overflow. Suddenly, I felt like everything was pointless. I thought, *I've been running, giving, and juggling my responsibilities, but nothing is working out. There's no better illustration of my life than this sign.*

Choking back tears, I turned the car around. I couldn't think of an alternative for our day out. I couldn't plan. I'd been feeling run down lately, physically overtaxed, overweight as I'd never been before— and recent events had left me mentally exhausted as well.

At the first gas station, I pulled over and called my parents. Sobbing, I whispered, "Please come. Something is not right with me."

All my life, I'd been strong. I was the one who made things happen. Divorced for twelve years, I'd made a life for myself and my girls on a nine-acre property outside of Asheville, North Carolina. I had twenty-six years of clinical experience in alternative health and energy healing, and worked with thousands of clients locally and around the world. I gave lectures, taught online courses, and ran workshops.

I thought I had the life I'd always wanted. So why did everything suddenly feel futile?

Looking back, I can see that the signs were there, but at the time I didn't see them that way. One of my employees, whom I'd considered a friend, had been double-billing me and taking money from my accounts, and I felt like my business partner was constantly climbing on my shoulders to get ahead. The constant need to be on guard was exhausting, and sapped the joy from my work.

After the day of our canceled lake visit, all I wanted to do was sleep. I fought the urge for a while, but it soon became stronger than I was.

I stayed in bed for a day, which turned into a week. A few weeks after that, I didn't know if I'd ever have the energy to get up again. No matter how much I slept, I still felt exhausted, hopeless, and empty. I ate at my mother's insistence, but I had no appetite. If I could have bored a hole in the mattress and disappeared forever, I would have.

My daughters knew where to find me. They would come into the bedroom and sit with me, or lie next to me and watch TV in silence. That was all I had the energy to do.

My mother got really worried, and insisted I have a physical. I was tempted to postpone those appointments, but she insisted. Some medical issues were discovered; nothing grave, just imbalances that could be corrected with proper nutrition, supplements, and pills. However, a DNA test showed that I have a methylation issue, and can't handle extreme amounts of stress.

After that, I stayed in bed for three months.

With proper nutrition and lots of love and support, my energy started to come back. I got up, got dressed, and decided that whatever I was dealing with was over. I was ready for the next chapter in my life.

Not so fast.

For the next year or so, I worked remotely for different companies. I didn't want to come back to my old profession, which I felt had been overtaken by charlatans. But I still felt empty and disengaged, like I was just going through the motions. Plus, I was still dealing with my darkness: my ego, my weak places, my inconsistency as a high frequency being. I had a lot to iron out.

And then, one morning, eighteen months later, I woke up with a major "a-ha!" God had spoken to me. He told me it was time to come back, and do the work I was meant to do. The call was so strong, it felt like a thousand or more voices were asking, inviting, and welcoming me back.

I knew, then, that I had been brought to my knees so that I could come back to my work with greater grace and integrity.

I wasn't prepared for the firestorm that ensued. Many in my industry were shocked and disappointed that I had returned. They had thought their way was clear. I found myself in the middle of a multimillion-dollar lawsuit against another healer/practitioner who had stolen my program while I was recovering, and pursuing a former employee for violating her non-compete, non-disclosure clause. In my absence, my years of experience were lied about, my illness was viciously gossiped about, and my character was assassinated. These vicious lies and rumors, coming as they did from people who had formerly pledged their allegiance and love, were heartbreaking.

It was during that time of reemergence that my story of gratitude and grace really began. I had a choice, as we all do: I could buy into the image that others were selling of me, or hold fast to the lessons I had learned in my time away. I chose the latter.

I know, now, who I am. I know how strong I am, and that I am surrounded by love and support. I was put on this earth to give, to help, to heal—and no one can take away that God-given purpose. Instead of listening to the rumors and gossip, I choose to hear the loving voices of the friends and clients who prayed for my return.

It's been a year since I came back to my healing work—a very active, gratifying, successful year. I am teaching brand new information about natural health and how energy technology connects to medicine. I've been interviewed on mainstream media and radio, created powerful programs, and networked with healers and practitioners all over the world. I've earned more money than I ever have before, and I've given more money away.

What I've discovered is that the full realization of grace cannot happen until you've experienced its opposite. Most of us have seen the darkness in divorce, business failures, and family struggles, but few of us have chosen to be grateful for these challenges as the gifts they are, and celebrate them as a path to grace.

You can't run from yourself or your life—but, as I discovered, you can choose to build a new one, with gratitude.

Reflection

Kimberly needed to be brought to the brink before she recognized the places within her that needed healing. What can you do today to address the issues you've been avoiding?

_____

_____

_____

_____

What has been the "fallout" from your inner growth, and how are you stronger for it?

_____

_____

_____

_____

If you built a new life based totally on gratitude, what would it look like?

_____

_____

_____

_____

My Dirty Little Secret

Dr. Mary E. Pritchard, PhD, HHC

I had just turned forty, broken my heel for the second time in a year, gotten a divorce, and moved into a new home when a friend of mine confronted me about my dirty little secret.

"You have an eating disorder," he said.

"No," I retorted. "I *study* eating disorders; I don't have one." After all, by that point, I had been researching factors that cause body dissatisfaction and eating disorders in both men and women for nearly twenty years.

"That doesn't mean you don't have one," my friend said.

Over the course of the next week, I fought with him, denied, blame-shifted, raged … and finally gave in. Despite the fact that I was on crutches, in a cast, and hadn't worked for six months because of my broken heel, I was steadily losing weight. I was a shell of the woman I had once been. When I looked in the mirror, I saw a woman I loathed—a woman I was ashamed of. All of the things I had identified myself as had been steadily stripped away. I was no longer a wife, I couldn't run or work out, and, at the time, I was on sabbatical from my position as a university professor, so I wasn't even working my full-time job. I didn't know who I was anymore, but one thing was crystal clear: I wasn't healthy. I had a problem, and I needed help.

I booked an appointment with a therapist. As I walked in the door, she said, "So, you have an eating disorder."

"Yes," I admitted. "Yes, I do."

When I first started to heal my eating disorder, I felt lost. On the one hand, I was determined to "beat" my eating disorder. I *had* to beat it: I was the researcher, not the victim. If I couldn't heal myself, would that mean I was a fraud? A loser? A failure?

On the other hand, my eating disorder had been my primary coping mechanism for twenty-four years. Living without it, I felt like I was trying to ask for directions in Latin: I couldn't talk about it, because I didn't think anyone would understand. Most of all, though, I was ashamed that the very disease I spoke so passionately about, and researched to prevent, had taken its toll on me.

Even after I admitted I had a problem and sought help, I was still in denial. It took a few months of seeing my treatment team on a regular basis for me to finally admit how insidious and invasive my eating disorder had become.

It was so sneaky, so good at convincing me that I was healing when I clearly wasn't. It whispered things like: "I know your therapist told you not to exercise, but she meant don't run." "Lifting weights and using the elliptical machine are okay, because strong bones and cardiovascular exercise make you healthy." "You're not restricting food intake; your body just doesn't process fat very well since you had your gall bladder removed." "It's okay if you eat oatmeal every day for breakfast and dinner; it's easy to prepare. And it's not like you can cook—you have a broken heel!"

I remember when I first confessed my dirty little secret to my best friend. "I have an eating disorder," I blurted out.

"Yes," she said. "I know. I thought you knew and just didn't want to talk about it."

Apparently the only person I had been fooling was myself. My illness was the big pink elephant in the room that everyone saw, but didn't want to talk about.

After that, I dove in headfirst—for real this time. I decided I was going to beat this thing. That worked for a few months—right up until I started dating a man who was a recovering bulimic.

I know, I know. Why would I date someone else who had a problem with food? My reasoning was that he'd get me, that he'd understand what I was going through. I thought we could keep each other on track with our recovery, but that wasn't what happened. My problem was too deeply seated, too ingrained; his had been fleeting. At the first sign of stress in our relationship, I did what I knew how to do: I restricted my food intake. I fell back into the comforting arms of my eating disorder, and stayed in that hole for two months.

I got sick. *Really* sick. Four head colds in a month, followed by a bout of walking pneumonia that wouldn't let go and an abnormal EKG that had my eating disorder treatment team up in arms. Two rounds of antibiotics, a round of steroids, a pulmonary embolism scare (which turned out to be negative) and two blood draws later, I still couldn't seem to kick the cough and chest pains.

I was making dinner for my boyfriend, hacking and holding my chest to keep the pains in check, when he looked at me and asked, quizzically, "Are you okay?" As though he'd just now noticed how sick I was. As though the abnormal EKG and pulmonary embolism scare were minor, insignificant bumps in the road.

"No," I replied. "I'm not okay."

"Oh."

That was all he had to say on the subject. After wolfing down his dinner, he headed out for the night to spend the evening with his friends.

A few days later, I relayed my frustration about this to my best friend. "I am clearly sick," I lamented. "Why can't he make dinner for a change, or stay home and take care of me?"

My friend, a big believer in Louise Hay's *You Can Heal Your Life,* said, "Why do you think you're having chest pains?"

Put off by what seemed to be a tangent in our conversation, I bit back a snappy reply, and considered. Why *was* I having chest pains? What was really happening with me?

"My heart is breaking," I said. "This relationship is killing me."

She nodded sagely. "You know what you have to do."

It took me another two weeks to work up the courage to do it—but on the day I kicked my boyfriend out of my house, my chest pains vanished. Once again, I began to climb out of the hole of my eating disorder. It took me a few months, but I got there. And I have never been more grateful.

What I've learned from my eating disorder is this: life is a series of choices. Sometimes, our choices are clear enough for us to see how they affect the course of our lives—like when I chose to admit I needed help. And sometimes, our refusal to choose is a choice, too—like when I kept putting off breaking up with my boyfriend because I was afraid that I was so broken and flawed that I would never meet anyone better.

I don't regret either one of them.

You see, I am a firm believer that life happens *for* us, not *to* us. Every single day, we have so much to be grateful for: the good, and the not-so-good. Every choice we make (or refuse to make) teaches us something we need to learn and understand about ourselves, life, and the Universe.

As I started the latest phase of my recovery, I began to ask myself the tough questions: What did I learn from my twenty-four-year battle with "almost-anorexia"? What did I learn from my failed romantic relationships? Why did those things happen for me, and what lessons were they trying to teach me?

Then, I had to forgive myself.

To me, forgiveness is letting go of the hope that the past could have been any different than it was. It was time to stop blaming myself for my eating disorder, and for making poor choices when it came to romantic relationships. I had to let it all go.

Finally, I had to learn to love myself enough to make different choices. It's not that I never make mistakes—after all, mistakes are God's way of giving us a do-over, so that next time we actually get it right—but as soon as I realized what I've done, I dust myself off, forgive myself, and move on.

My new life formula is working quite well. At forty-two, I'm happier and healthier than I've ever been. I haven't fallen back in the hole of my eating disorder since the day I re-committed to healing. Even better, I now have the tools and experience to help other women heal in a big way, figure out their life lessons, learn to forgive and love themselves, and realize their own self-worth.

I am so grateful. Every single day, I am so grateful.

What's your dirty little secret—the one thing you've never wanted to admit to anyone?

_____

_____

_____

_____

What do you think would happen if your secret was no longer a secret?

_____

_____

_____

_____

What would your life be like if you could forgive yourself for the things that cause you shame or fear?

_____

41

_____

_____

_____

CHAPTER
Two

Grace is ...
Releasing The Past

A Poem About War

Peggy Nolan

*W*e swarm the plane as
The returning heroes disembark
I search the crowd for my husband
They all look the same
In chocolate chip uniforms

A stranger hoists Christina on her shoulders
From her higher vantage point
She spots him first and squeals

The noise of the crowd fades
My husband home from the war
Hugs both our daughters
And captures me with his smile and mouths
"I love you."

"*No!*" I screamed inside my head. "*It doesn't end like that. He cheated. He lied!*" I wanted to rip the notebook paper in front of me to shreds.

My hands shook as I looked at the squiggly lines that formed letters into words—squiggles that were not of me, but came through me in one rush.

These squiggles painted words faster than I could think them. My pen only stopped when the rush that flowed from my brain and through my right shoulder, took a ninety-degree turn at my elbow, sped through my wrist, and finally gushed out through my fingertips.

Just as I was about to rip the offending pages from my notebook, something pushed me away from the kitchen table. I know it was me pushing away—but at the same time, it wasn't.

I stood up and walked around my kitchen. I touched the chairs of my new kitchen set. I opened the fridge and stared vacantly, searching for something that I knew wasn't in there.

This was the home I'd moved into after my divorce: after I sold the house we'd shared, after I sold all the furniture, after I purged myself of all physical traces of a nineteen-year marriage.

Divorce cut clear through my family, and left a gaping hole in my heart. While I was engrossed in feelings of rage and revenge, my children were sliced and diced like onions in a Ron Popeil chopper. Everything my girls knew to be safe and secure disintegrated right before their eyes. The people they counted on flaked out. *I* flaked out. It didn't matter who was right or who was wrong; in what felt like an instant, the bubble had burst, and no one was left steering the ship. My daughters weren't just angry, they were scared.

So was I.

I worked on getting my act together, not just for me, but for my girls as well. But no matter how good I made things look on the outside, on the inside I was still pointing fingers, blaming my ex for just about everything. No matter what I did, at the end of the day I went to bed with a hot pit of anger raging inside. Bitter and cynical, I plastered a smile across my face—only to have someone I barely knew see beyond the mask and call me out.

The Pink Lipstick Lady

"How often do your girls see their dad?" she asked, as she tied a bow on the organza gift bag.

I squirmed, not liking the question all that much. "As often as they want."

I could tell that she wasn't being nosy on purpose, but I felt irritated anyway. She continued to make conversation as we worked on the gift bags for the women's conference.

"How far away does he live?"

"Five miles." I noticed her bright pink lipstick, and imagined how it would look smeared across her face after I sucker-punched her. I tossed another gift bag in the box. One down, only one hundred fifty to go.

My insides started to broil. *Why did I agree to help get the gift bags ready? This chick can leave any time. Now would be good. Right now. Now-now-now-now!*

"Oh sweetie," she chirped. "I don't mean to pry, but you're carrying a huge grudge."

I shook my head. "Nope. I'm not carrying a grudge." Who, me? *Oh, nooooooo. Not me, not me, not me.*

She stopped what she was doing, and put her hand on her hip. Her bright blue eyes pierced through my skin like laser beams. "You most certainly are, honey," she waggled her finger at me. "Your whole body *screams* grudge."

My eyes narrowed. "What are you talking about?"

Bring it on sweetie. You wanna fight? I'll smack that pink lipstick right off your mouth.

Pink Lipstick Lady never raised her voice, never wavered from being a kind, curious observer. "Your whole face squished up in disgust. You crossed your arms. Your entire body tensed up." She tied off another gift bag and dropped it in the box.

I looked down and noticed my crossed arms. *Release!* My arms dropped to my sides. "No," I said, softer this time. "I'm not holding a grudge."

But I was. Pink Lipstick Lady had seen right through me. A colossal boulder sat on my shoulder, and I desperately wanted her to leave so I could be alone with it.

My grudge didn't go away overnight just because someone had called me on it. No. It stuck around, out in the open, no longer hidden, a constant reminder of the war raging inside my head and heart. Pink Lipstick Lady made me aware of it—but it would take another cosmic 2x4, disguised as a writing assignment, to pulverize the grudge once and for all.

A Poem About War

I read the assignment. It made as much sense to me as rhyming something with orange, or trying to smell the number nine: "Write a poem about war."

Really? Are there any good war poems out there? What the hell?

Flashes of light went off in my head. Neurons exploded on synaptic wires. And I literally saw the light—the headlight of a 747 jet airliner coming closer and closer. The pen in my hand began to write, and for nine wrenching pages it didn't stop.

> *A deep voice over the PA*
> *Announces, "Plane's on approach.*
> *It's twenty miles out."*

> *A cheer ripples through the crowd*
> *Family members, townspeople, the media*
> *Welcoming home four hundred members of the*
> *357th Tactical Fighter Wing*

> *America's Gulf War veterans*
> *One of them—my husband*
> *A man I haven't seen in 210 days*

I remembered it all: Iraq's invasion of Kuwait, the call for the A-10 Thunderbolt, the aircraft my husband worked on. I remembered the day he hugged us goodbye, all of us wondering if we'd ever see each other again. Scud missiles. No communication. Writing letters every day. I held down the home front, raised our daughters, and entertained his mother on Christmas Day.

The words I wrote fell into place, one after the other. The day the Gulf War started, I checked in with my band of military wives. We stayed on the line with each other, glued to our TVs as CNN brought the war to us, live, without commercial interruptions.

The poem that poured out of me took me by surprise. A snapshot in time, a remembering of love, longing, and intense waiting.

I hated it. I wanted to crumple it up and throw it away. I wanted to burn it.

Most of all I hated how it ended, with my ex-husband returning home from the First Gulf War and telling me he loved me. *Why does he get off the hook?* I screamed inside my head.

My body tensed with anger. As I went to scribble out the last sentence, a voice from nowhere and everywhere said to me, *"Put the pen down."*

I put the pen down and pushed away from the table. As I looked around my kitchen and my surroundings, bewildered, the voice spoke again. *"He loved you once and you loved him. Remember that. Remember love."*

I didn't want to remember that. I didn't want to remember the truth that he had loved me once, and that I had loved him. I had gotten used to my anger, and used to hating him. I was afraid that my dark cloud of despair would leave. Would I be strong enough to let go and move forward without my armor of self-righteous bravado and hatred?

Who would I be without this tale of woe, this wound?

I stood there, next to my kitchen table, for a long time—long enough for my inner temper tantrum to subside. And that's when I sensed something else, something I hadn't felt for a long time.

A calmness bubbled up from deep inside me. I felt surrounded by warmth and love. For the first time in years I experienced a sense of freedom and quiet peace. Everything seemed to shift and open up as I physically felt the release of my hatred towards my ex.

The war in my head and in my heart went silent. The persistent churn of anger, resentment, and blame that raged inside me vanished. The grudge exposed by Pink Lipstick Lady was now gone, smashed to smithereens by the forgiving memory of love, and a poem about war.

49

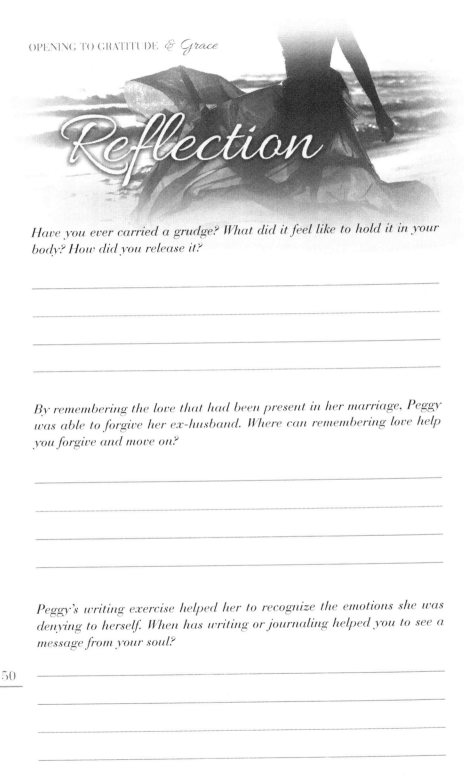

Reflection

Have you ever carried a grudge? What did it feel like to hold it in your body? How did you release it?

_____

_____

_____

_____

By remembering the love that had been present in her marriage, Peggy was able to forgive her ex-husband. Where can remembering love help you forgive and move on?

_____

_____

_____

_____

Peggy's writing exercise helped her to recognize the emotions she was denying to herself. When has writing or journaling helped you to see a message from your soul?

_____

_____

_____

_____

Virgin Snow

Cindy Hively

"**I**s all this *really* happening?" I asked the air, smiling in amazement.

It felt like a dream. My dad had just finished helping me unload the last of my few belongings, showed me how to check all the fluids in my car (again), and reminded me about how to keep a budget and a checkbook. Now, I was sitting on my bed in my new studio apartment in this great big mansion, and it was *a-ma-zing.*

The space was huge. There were floor-to-ceiling windows on three walls; I felt like I was in a sunny greenhouse. I practiced a few times throwing open the eight sets of flowing drapes, like in the movies.

It was May of 1986, and I was the luckiest girl in the world. Everything was falling into place. In four days, I would be graduating from college. I'd already landed a job as a manager of La Vogue, one of the area's poshest retail stores. My dad had helped me find a car, and now I had this cinema-worthy space to call home. I was fabulous, carefree, and totally excited for the next adventure to unfold.

One of my best friends from college lived close by, and every day we talked or went on an adventure of some kind. We were due to go shopping and have dinner on this sunny Saturday afternoon. I was the only resident in this upstairs section of the house, so it wasn't a big deal for me to vacuum the sitting area in my underwear. Why get my clothes dirty?

There I was in my lacy bra and panties, vacuuming and singing away, when I suddenly had the sense that I wasn't alone. I turned my head to the right and ...

51

"Holy cow!" I screeched. Two guys I'd never seen before were standing there, watching me with half-embarrassed looks on their faces. I dashed into my room, pulled the vacuum cord out of the wall, and slammed the door.

An hour or so later, I emerged. I was hoping I'd be alone—but there he was, my new neighbor, with his arms full of boxes.

I blushed like crazy, and he laughed. The sparks we both felt could have burned the place down.

I arrived home that evening to find a note taped to my door, asking for the use of a hammer and a good set of eyes. I laughed to myself. "Yeah, what girl *doesn't* have a tool set?"

Actually, I was the only girl I knew who actually owned a toolbox, thanks again to my dad. I grabbed my hammer, ventured across the hall, and knocked softly on the door. My cheeks and neck were already flushing. I knocked a little harder.

The door opened, and for the next four hours Myles and I listened to records and got to know one another. We did a little kissing. (Okay, we did a *lot* of kissing.) Over the next few weeks, our casual meetings turned into cooking meals together, taking nightly walks, and sharing from the deepest parts of our souls. We shared everything: our dreams, our desires, and our difficulties.

Myles was my first love. He was my protector, and he kept me safe as I ventured into the world as an adult. We had a secret hiding place in the breaker box where he would leave poems and love notes for me. Although the paper has yellowed and torn, I still have these poems and notes today.

There was one cloud hanging over our relationship, though: I was still engaged to marry Rich, my college boyfriend. A year into my relationship with Myles, I broke things off—but there was a force around Rich that wouldn't allow me to let him go completely. We had been college sweethearts, and our life together had been preordained long before Myles came into the picture.

Two years later, my wedding was in the works, and it was time to say farewell to my first real love.

I remember packing up my studio apartment, boxing up the life I'd created there. Myles came over to help, and said something to me that I've come to understand even more deeply over the years: "We will always love each other in a way that is unexplainable. If we need one another, we will know it, and feel it, no matter where we are in the world."

I choked back the tears and nodded. "Yes."

Our goodbye was one of the most painful moments of either of our lives. We held each other and cried for almost an hour, not saying much.

We kept our promise to one another, and spoke several times a year for the next two decades. Myles supported me through my divorce from Rich, career difficulties, and other huge life changes. When he found a woman to marry a few years after my divorce, I was happy for him—and when I met the new love of my life, and married him, it made things easier to know that Myles was as happy as I was. We had shared true love, and now we had both found it again with other people.

Then, for no reason I can think of, we lost contact.

For eight long years, I didn't speak to or hear from Myles. Then, one cold January day this past year, I was working and posting on Facebook when a message popped up. It was a friend request from Myles, dated August 2012.

How had it taken nearly four years for this message to reach me? It was a divine message of some kind. Things like this didn't just happen out of the blue. Intrigued, I accepted the request, and sent him a quick note to apologize for the fact that it had taken me so long to reach out.

On Myles's personal page, there wasn't a lot of information. His picture was there, and some information about a project he was working on. Then, a feeling like ice came over me. Something wasn't right; I could feel it. It wasn't intellectual, but it was powerful.

I Googled Myles's name, and clicked on the first link I saw. I wasn't prepared for what came up.

I was looking at his obituary. He had passed away in 2013.

It dropped me to the floor. For fifteen minutes, the tears flowed. I couldn't make sense of his passing. He had only been forty-nine! He'd stayed in shape, and was a huge advocate of wellness practices. In fact, he'd been working out on a treadmill when he collapsed. He never regained consciousness, and when it was determined that he had no brain activity, his wife had to make the terrible decision to take him off life support.

I started researching his life in 2012 and 2013, and began to understand why he'd been trying to reach out to me. He'd been trying to let me know that he was publishing his first book of poetry. The title of his book was *Virgin Snow*—the same title as the first poem he'd ever penned for me. It was about one of our nighttime walks together, when we held hands and felt no cold because of the fire in our hearts for one another. I still have the yellowed, handwritten copy that he'd left in the breaker box for me.

But why was I discovering this now? What was the lesson Myles was trying to send me from the realms of spirit?

A few days later, the answer was illuminated. I realized that we don't know how much we touch one another in life. Our impact can last for years, or for a single moment. Grace is a state of being that brings to light the true nature of gratitude—and each step into that grace is a step into virgin snow.

I'm not sure what my life would have been like if I'd stayed with Myles. Life is uncertain at best. We may have parted ways for unknown reasons, or lived happily ever after. I'll admit, I toyed with the "what ifs" for a while after I received his message. At the time, I was having some difficulties in my marriage, and for a few moments I allowed my heart to wander down those paths of memory—but I had a heart adjustment very quickly. Myles's message to me wasn't that I should lose myself in those snowy walks of the past, but that I should appreciate my husband and family more than ever.

After that day when I learned of Myles's death, I saw my husband differently. I saw his goodness and love, and the flaws started to diminish. I went from looking at all the "wrongness" to seeing all that was beautiful and right with my man and my marriage. I realized how much I was loved, in spite of—or maybe *because* of—my imperfections. The grace of that love is the same grace that God gives me: it's unconditional.

Now, when I read "Virgin Snow," I am grateful beyond words to Myles, not only for the love he showed me back then, but for the gift of gratitude that changed my life thirty-four years later.

Who was your first true love? In what ways did he or she shape your life?

_____

_____

_____

_____

_____

In what ways has your understanding of love evolved over the years?

_____

_____

_____

_____

_____

Myles' spiritual message to Cindy changed the way she looked at her marriage. Where can you shift your views to see the good in those you love, instead of the faults?

_____

_____

_____

_____

Broken Open

Mal Duane

*T*his year, I ended my marriage to the man I once believed to be my soulmate.

Never in a million years did I think that divorce would be a possibility for us. But guess what? Life happens.

Flashback ...

After being single for many years, I had finally met the most perfect individual for me. I was marrying a man who really saw me for the strong, purposeful, and yet sometimes vulnerable woman I am. He loved the woman who had embraced long-term recovery, and who lived her burning desire to help other women be their best selves.

I felt an emotional bond with this man—but I felt an even deeper soul connection. We were meant for one another. There was a soul contract between us. And so, we married.

I grew in this relationship. My vision to help women expanded into writing a book, coaching women, and sharing my inspiration with those who needed it through a multitude of social media channels. I became a stepmother—and a grandmother, which is something I never thought I would experience. I was inspired to be more, to do more, never suspecting that all the while my husband was engaged in something dark and demeaning to me as his wife, and as a woman.

You know the expression: "Life can change in a minute." Mine certainly did—on a day just after our ten-year anniversary, when the axe of betrayal landed sharply in the center of my ignorant bliss, and buried itself in the tender flesh of my naïve, loving heart.

I'm not really sure what prompted me to look for files on my husband's computer, but a small voice kept guiding me to do so. When

I finally sat down at the keyboard, I found a file that shocked me to my core. I wanted to run away, but my intuition told me that this was only the tip of the iceberg—and sure enough, it was.

I sat on the floor, breathless. I couldn't move. My head was pounding. It took almost thirty minutes before I could drag myself up the stairs to confront him.

Trying to behave like a superwoman, I stuffed my own feelings down deep at first. I told myself I could work through this—that I could fix it. I was locked into survival mode. Over the next eighteen months, I did everything from marriage counseling and individual therapy to support groups and spiritual coaching. I read a dozen different books on mending a broken heart, and studied every forgiveness practice I could find.

But as my head charged further and further ahead, my heart never caught up. I felt heavier and heavier—because deep down, I knew that my husband's dishonesty was still present. I felt it like a weight in my gut. Every time I was near him, my whole body tightened up.

I had come to the dreaded fork in the road. I had done all I could; now, it was time for me to make a different choice.

Betrayal is an old story, and it's always the same. It is committed by someone very close to you, someone whom you trust without question. The pain cuts so deeply that it paralyzes you at first. You feel like you are being thrown about in a bouncy-house whose walls are covered in shards of glass. You are being slashed to ribbons, and there is absolutely nothing you can do about it.

Wrong.

We always have the power to change our circumstances. But in order to do so, we have to take our power back, and be willing to walk a different path.

Even while I was moving through my process, I had unwavering faith that I would figure out the highest and best path for both myself and my husband. But the harder I tried to get some accountability from him, the more resistance I was met with. Finally, I had to admit that I was powerless over his behavior—or anyone else's, for that matter. I needed to shift my focus back onto myself and my own healing, cut all of the energetic cords that were holding me in fear and despair, and choose a new way.

I was sitting at my desk, listening to a video on *A Course in Miracles*, when it hit me: I was done. My husband wasn't really trying to save our marriage; he was just going through the motions to appease me. It was time for him to move out, and take the time and space to think about what he really wanted from our relationship. More, it was time for me to let go of the dream of our marriage and begin to heal my shattered heart.

I am grateful for all of my studies, which helped me to stay on the high road. I was mindful of everything I said and did. I negotiated a very good deal on his apartment lease, and spent two months packing his belongings, making sure he had everything he needed to be comfortable in his new home. There were over sixty boxes, along with enough furniture to fill the two-bedroom unit. He didn't need to buy a thing.

As I helped him unpack his things and organize his new kitchen, I knew in my heart that he would never be coming back to our marital home, but I still held a tiny flame of hope that we could create a new and different kind of relationship together. As time went on, though, I realized that friendly dinners and casual chats weren't an option for me. He wasn't interested in changing, and my heart was ready for complete closure. I had done my work, and fulfilled my part of our soul contract. There was nothing more for me to do. It was truly time to move on.

Looking back, I feel nothing but pride in myself for how I handled a difficult situation without attacking or being intentionally cruel to someone who betrayed me so completely. I carry no guilt today, and I don't wonder how I could have done more. He chose to stay where he was, and do what he did. I chose to grow.

As shocking as it was, I can honestly say that I am grateful to have learned the truth. Living with long-term, calculated dishonesty—even if I didn't know it was happening at the time—did not serve my soul or my heart's desire. I believe that my discovery that day was divinely orchestrated to free me from the toxic energy I was unconsciously immersed in, and bring me to a place of understanding and compassion.

The legal process of dissolving a marriage leaves a lot to be desired. Even if you enter with the best of intentions, it can easily become a combative situation. I was so hopeful for a peaceful ending through mediation, but it didn't work. Ultimately I had to stand up and advocate for myself. The day I went to court, my intention was the same as on the day I started the divorce process: I wanted fairness and accountability. In the end, that was what I got. It looked different than I thought it would, but the sense of peace I experienced in my body as I walked out of the courtroom told me that this was the perfect ending for me.

Today, I am filled with gratitude for my life. My home is bright and cheery again, and the smell of fresh lilies permeates my living room. I have repainted, recarpeted, and redecorated, and I've smudged every corner to bring in positive energy.

I admit, it's strange to be single again. When I got married, I thought it would be for the rest of my life. Now, the rest of my life is waiting for me along a new path—but I am stronger, wiser, and more loving than I was before, and I am not afraid.

Have you ever experienced betrayal? How did it change your life? What did you learn from it?

What would it take for you to forgive someone who has betrayed you? What would your life be like if you no longer carried that burden?

Mal writes about "choosing a new path." What new path can you choose to reclaim your power and self-love?

61

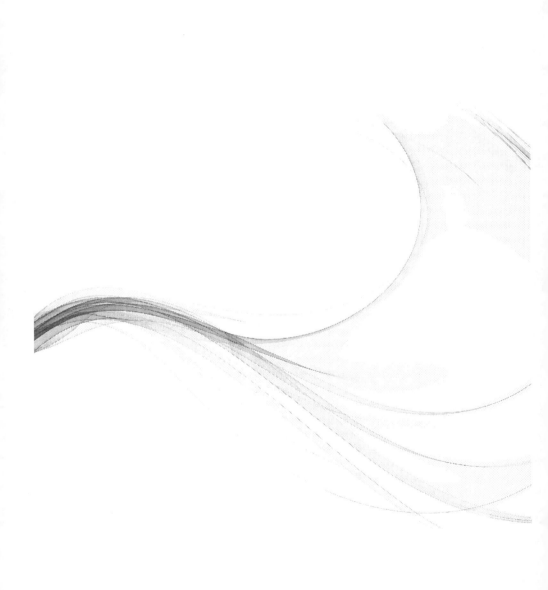

A Graceful Exit

Dr. Angela M. Joyner

*F*or weeks, I felt as if I was walking through a murky cloud. The tension at work was so thick that it felt as if I had been swaddled in a heavy, damp, woolen blanket. While most of us tried to carry on like it was "business as usual," it was anything but. The rumor mill was going full spin now and every day I heard another perspective about when "it" was going to happen.

I was committed to helping my team stay focused, energized and passionate about our business performance. We were on the verge of delivering the best performance our billion-dollar portfolio had ever seen. I felt a great deal of ownership for my piece of our Fortune 500 company, and was so proud of what we'd accomplished. Each person on the team had contributed to our success; their enthusiasm was a stark difference to what the rest of the organization was expressing.

Although I was pleased by the performance of my portfolio, I still had trouble sleeping through the night. With the threat of company-wide layoffs and restructuring hanging over my head, my mind was constantly racing when I should have been relaxing and recovering. I was self-medicating with junk food, *Golden Girls* re-runs, and Swedish Fish. I wanted to speed through time and *get through it already*—but at the same time, I felt safe in the moment.

And so, I did what I always do when I'm confused, uncertain, or in need of support: I prayed. I asked God to give me guidance. I expressed how grateful I was for my life, my accomplishments, my family, and my health. My life was incredibly rich! I had traveled to several continents, skydived, and earned several degrees. What I most needed now was peace and courage to face my uncertain future.

I asked God to calm my heart, close any door that was not meant for me, and open the ones that would lead to the next season of my life. The door slammed the very next day.

I received a phone call asking me to report to work for a confidential and mandatory meeting. I was scheduled to be at an agency meeting downtown, and had not planned to be in the office that day, but once I saw the urgent e-mail I called to confirm the request and immediately adjusted my plans.

When it came time for the meeting, I walked to the designated office and saw my boss waiting for me. What I didn't expect was that the HR manager was there as well. It was clear in that moment, before anyone had even spoken a word, that this chapter of my career was coming to a close.

I was told that my position was being eliminated as part of a major restructuring. There was more—but truthfully, after I heard the first few comments, I completely tuned out. I wanted nothing more than to leave the office, go home, and lie down. My face became extremely hot, and I realized that what I was feeling was not anger but embarrassment.

A million thoughts were running through my head. I understood that it was not about my performance; however, if I was performing so well, why was I not chosen to stay? Where had I fallen short? Why couldn't I continue to be a strong contributor in the new organization?

These questions continued to plague my mind on my forty-five-minute drive home.

I couldn't wait to be in the comfort and sanctuary of my home. Once I walked into my house, I collapsed on the couch, exhausted. After months of anticipating the inevitable layoff, it had finally come. I could breathe, and release the tension that I had been carrying. My parents and close friends offered to come over to support me, but what I wanted most was time to just "be."

My natural tendency when faced with adversity is to push through it and move on to the next thing. But this time, as my mind was busy trying to pull together a game plan, and tallying up all the lifestyle changes I'd need to make in order to stretch out my severance pay, my body simply shut down and refused to move.

I could cut out little luxuries, my mind chattered, *like high-end travel and shopping. I can be flexible.* But although I was already crafting Plan B, part of me knew that I needed to fully open to and embrace the emotions I was feeling.

This experience of "sitting with" my feelings would be critical for my growth. As I lay there, counting the elapsing minutes on my watch, I felt as if this chapter of my life was quickly slipping through my hands, like the sands in an hourglass. My emotions swung from fear, to grief, to hope, and then back to fear. Every once in a while I would feel a tinge of self-righteousness, shame, or indignation. When shame showed up, I felt as if I had let down a legacy of men and women who had paved the way for my career opportunities. When self-righteousness showed up, I became incensed that, despite my performance and dedication, the company no longer wanted me.

Right then, everything was fraught with contradiction. I needed to be alone, but longed to be embraced. I needed to know that my work mattered to my company, but I also wanted to run as fast as I could into my next chapter. I wanted support, but not the usual empty platitudes like, "You're going to be okay."

It became very clear over the next several days who really understood me and what I needed, and who didn't.

When I returned to work for my last two weeks, I felt like a dead woman walking. Everyone was dealing with the layoffs in their own way, trying to make sense out of it all. Most people didn't say anything to me; some even avoided eye contact. I was gently uninvited to meetings, and suddenly my calendar, which had once been filled to the brim, became clear.

All I wanted was for the days to speed by, but they passed painstakingly, at a snail's pace. The more I wanted to rush through the pain, discomfort, and confusion, the longer the days dragged on. Part of me wished I could just toss my hands in the air and stop coming to work. But even if my presence for the transition process hadn't been required as part of my severance package, I still would have continued to show up. This might have been the end of my job, but it certainly wasn't the end of my career. I wanted to model to my team and peers that I was stronger than any title or position, and end my time with the company the same way I'd begun it: with integrity.

I held my head high for the entire two weeks. Inside, though, what I really wanted was silence, solitude, and to feel like I mattered. I needed to be held, cherished, and adored. I prayed for courage, guidance, and love.

I prayed for a graceful exit.

My prayers were more than answered. After those first awkward days, when people were still trying to process the layoffs and all that they implied, I received amazing support from my coworkers and friends. I was overwhelmed by the raw emotion that others showed about my departure. Their words comforted me, and I felt embraced by their wishes for a bright future.

As I soaked in everything around me during those final days, one emotion started to emerge from the inner turmoil: it was gratitude. I was grateful for the people who had poured into my professional and personal life. My memories of the smiles, words of wisdom, and laughter began to fill me with joy. I was grateful for the time I spent at my company and all of the wonderful things that I had achieved. My life had been ridiculously blessed by my career, and by the people who I'd had the honor of meeting. My coworkers had become my surrogate family in Chicago, filling the void caused by the geographical distance between me and my family in Atlanta.

At last, buoyed by love and gratitude, I realized that God was closing this door because he had something greater for me to do. This season of my life and career was ending so that I could use my gifts differently. I couldn't move on to my next chapter while I was defiantly holding on to the last one.

Deep in my soul, I knew that God was preparing me for more. He had given me glimpses of what could be in store for me, and the possibilities were astounding!

On my last day, I wrote letters to everyone who'd had a meaningful impact on my career, and told my team how much they mattered to me. I didn't want to move forward without saying how grateful I was to have shared this time with them.

When I woke up the next morning, I greeted the day with gratitude and joy. I knew it was the first day of a season of self-discovery, healing, possibilities, and reflection, and I was ready to greet my future with grace and gratitude.

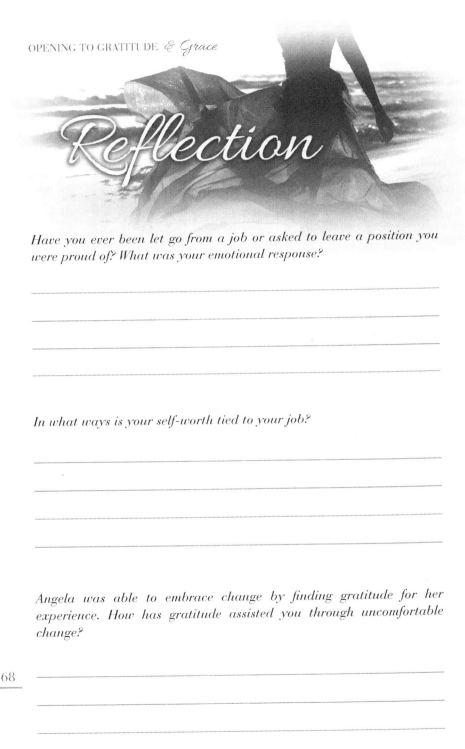

Reflection

Have you ever been let go from a job or asked to leave a position you were proud of? What was your emotional response?

_____

_____

_____

_____

In what ways is your self-worth tied to your job?

_____

_____

_____

_____

Angela was able to embrace change by finding gratitude for her experience. How has gratitude assisted you through uncomfortable change?

_____

_____

_____

_____

My Out-of-the-Box Life

Stacey Hoffer

*I*n October of 2013, I flew to Northern California to attend my very first women's circle retreat. As the circle opened, one of our leaders asked us to close our eyes, open our hearts, and answer the question, "What do you want to receive from this retreat?"

The answer that surfaced immediately was *stillness*. I was craving stillness. Everything in my life was moving so fast; I felt like a disastrously uncoordinated juggler, dropping balls everywhere I turned. I wanted the chaos that had somehow taken over my life to be removed so I could just slow down and breathe.

"I'm going to ask you again," the retreat leader said. "This time, I want you to go deeper. What do you want to receive from this retreat?"

This time, the answer was louder. Words flowed out of me and onto the page of my journal. *I want to burn this box of a life that I feel completely trapped in. I want to stop feeling suffocated. I want to release everything that no longer serves me. I want to be free to live outside of the lines, and have space in my life to fully spread my wings.*

My "box of a life" was the life that I had unconsciously created. From the outside looking in, everything was beautiful. I'd left my corporate job to start my own business. I had a beautiful house, a husband, and two healthy children. I was living the dream—but the dream wasn't fully aligned with my heart and soul.

Before I went on this retreat, I knew something was missing, but I didn't know what it was. I only knew that I felt jailed, like there was an invisible chain holding me back from the life I truly desired.

After sharing what had come up for us as a result of the initial question, we separated into groups of three and intimately shared some of the old stories that were holding us back, running our lives, and no longer serving us. We were invited to put these old stories into the "alchemical fire" and turn them into gold.

When it was my turn to share, I opened my raw, vulnerable heart and said, "I'm not fully living in the way my soul desperately wants to live! I'm so busy trying to do everything I think I'm *supposed* to do, instead of trusting and living in alignment with my inner wisdom. It's exhausting, and it makes me feel bound and caged."

My inner wisdom knew I wanted a sacred partnership with my husband instead of a traditional marriage. It knew having deep soul-to-soul connections with my children was more important than being the "perfect mom" who always washed dishes after dinner and kept up with the laundry. It knew I needed more spaciousness in every aspect of my life. At the same time, those old, "logical" stories playing in my mind were telling me I had to be more organized, make more money, be more responsible, do what was expected of me, and be happy with the status quo.

I felt so trapped by these old stories. I knew it—but whenever they surfaced in my daily life, I would automatically go into fight-or-flight mode. It was not pretty, and I was not happy. It was time to make a change once and for all.

Day One of the retreat ended with a "burn and release" ceremony. I wrote down all of the old stories that were holding me hostage, and released them into the fire. We were given a mantra which I still use to this day: "I surrender. I receive. I surrender. I receive." I chanted these words over and over as my stories burned to ash.

In those moments, I surrendered my attachment to these self-sabotaging stories, and consciously chose love over fear. I opened the door of my cage, and let grace in.

Later, as I lay in bed with the moonlight on my blanket, a layer of calmness settled over me—a sense of peace that felt like coming home. All of my problems still needed to be solved, but something felt different. After years of feeling stagnated and trapped, I was taking baby steps onto my freedom path. I couldn't see the path clearly yet, and I had no idea where it would lead, but I knew in my heart that I had shifted into motion.

When I woke up the next morning, before getting out of bed, I asked the Universe to show me the next step along my freedom path, and to give me the courage to take that step. I asked the Universe to co-create new stories with me—stories that would fill my heart with joy, and allow my soul to soar. I ended this little conversation with the words, "I surrender the old stories that no longer serve me, and receive a new way of being that is in full alignment with my heart and soul."

I spent the next hour journaling, and engaging in a conversation with my heart and soul. "I see you," I gently told myself. "I am here, and from this day forward, I promise to give you permission to freely be *you*. I promise to carve out time for your dreams and desires. I promise to fully break you out of this caged box that I mistakenly put you in. And from this day forward, I promise to be guided by my heart, and no longer by fear. I don't have all the answers, but I promise to listen to my inner wisdom every step of the way."

Over the rest of that retreat, I started to get clearer about what it would mean to align with my heart and soul, live my life by my own rules, and shine my radiant inner light no matter what. I also found myself receiving the stillness I'd asked for at the very beginning of the retreat. I slowed down my breathing and my mind chatter, and allowed my inner wisdom and grace to emerge.

On the last night of the retreat, as our group sat under the full moon, I took my turn with the talking stick that was being passed around. Firmly, I declared: "I surrender not speaking and sharing my truth, and choose to take back my uncaged, unhinged, unedited, out-of-the-box life right now!"

The next morning, Sunday, I took a few moments to let it all sink in before heading back to my "real" life. I closed my eyes, emptied my mind, put my hand on heart, and tapped into my inner wisdom. With grace and ease, I heard the following guidance: *"Walk slowly. Walk boldly. Walk in the world with a full heart. I will carry you on my wings. I will keep you safe. We are now one heart. We have many more steps to walk, dear one—many, many more steps. They will not all be easy, but together we will move with ease and grace. Be free my love. I am here. Be free to love with all of your heart."*

That whisper from my inner wisdom gave me a glimpse of what was possible if I continued to listen to the whispers of my heart and soul. I still didn't have all the answers, and I still could not fully see the path I was choosing to walk, but I was already in possession of the gifts of *grace* and *choice*. As I said my farewells and left the retreat, I knew I was at a crossroads: I could choose to continue living with a closed heart, or I could choose to open my heart wider than I even imagined possible.

When I returned home, I started a daily practice of quieting my mind and envisioning my body as a vessel for divine love. I immediately noticed that, when I started making choices that were aligned with my inner wisdom, I was able to experience more harmony in my life. I've been doing this daily practice for over two years now, and it has fundamentally transformed my life.

Do my old stories still try to creep back in? Yes, they do. I'm not sure if they will ever truly go away. But now, I have the tools and practices in place to quiet them. More, I know I have a choice about whether to listen to them. Instead of feeling caged, I can now lovingly acknowledge these old states of being, and move beyond them to an elevated state of grace.

Where in your life do you feel "boxed in"?

_____

_____

_____

_____

If you could let go of your stories and "shoulds," what would your life look like? What would you do that you're not doing now?

_____

_____

_____

_____

Stacey writes about "the gifts of grace and choice." Where do grace and choice intersect in your life? What choices can you make right now to open your heart and embrace your life?

_____

73

_____

_____

_____

The Sanctuary

Laura Clark

Standing on the stoop, I wasn't sure what direction to take. *Déjà vu* consumed me. It was a time of celebration—but at the same time, I sensed something wrong.

The question came back to me, as it had before: "Was this the right decision?"

Fifteen years earlier, I stood on this same stoop, having just signed the papers to purchase my townhouse. I was proud of myself, and felt like celebrating, but doubts came up, too. Was this the right decision? Would I be able to handle the responsibility and the payments? My business was only two years young; would it continue to succeed?

I put the key in the lock, held my breath, and opened the door. I knew we—my townhouse and I—were in this together. As I began to move in, I allowed myself to appreciate the symbolism of independence that home ownership gave me.

My townhouse surrounded me with the energy I was seeking. She suited me well, and gave me the space to nurture myself, which in turn allowed me to step into a deeper understanding of who I was. No longer did I envision the family and the white picket fence; now, I saw the life of a strong, independent woman, with this space as her personal sanctuary.

Over time, she became a safe haven for others. My beloved Labrador twins, Tali and Tarsi, made this their first home. They chased each other, creating a race track through the bushes in the backyard, and provided me with endless hours of giggles. They also taught me true patience as they learned to come, sit, and stay.

My townhouse would later become a sanctuary for my father as well. After my mother transitioned forward, he and his dog joined me for a few years. I will always cherish this time we had. The townhouse provided the two of us with a safe place to really connect. We were able to deepen our respect for one another as adults while still maintaining our precious father-daughter relationship. He truly saw me as the vibrant, independent woman I had become.

The greatest gift by far that my townhouse gave, though, was the space to kindle and grow my relationship with my boyfriend, Michael. We had begun dating a few months before I purchased her and, at the time, becoming deeply involved with anyone was the last thing I desired. The townhouse allowed us *space*: space to discover who we both were at our core; space to understand each other's deepest dreams and desires; space to create the foundation for a life together. She was the greatest gift to our blossoming relationship.

Eventually, Dad moved home, and it was time for Michael and me to allow our relationship to grow under one roof. It was only natural for me to move into his home. He had built it himself. It was a halfway point between our respective workplaces, and the riverfront property was a great place for Tali, Tarsi, and his two dogs to run and play. It was the right home for becoming a family, and being in this life together.

This decision also meant that, after eight wonderful years, it was time for the townhouse to serve another purpose. And so, she shifted into being an income property for me—for us. On paper, this made sense, as her seaside town was always ripe for good rental units. But, as we discovered, she did not like having tenants. She was vacant, on and off, for two of the next six years. She had tenants who were wonderful but short-lived. She had tenants who treated her poorly.

This created negative energy everywhere. Each time we had to fix her up and get her ready for the next tenant, it took up valuable time and resources. She became an energetic drain on our financial resources, and was the cause for many disagreements between Michael and me. We thought things had shifted when we unexpectedly received new tenants who wanted to rent her long term. We were thrilled—but not for long, as these tenants grossly overstepped the rental agreements. I received complaint after complaint from neighbors. After four short months, I decided I'd had it with their antics.

Disagreements became arguments as Michael and I struggled with how to proceed. It was clear that evicting the tenants was the only way to get them out, but the law worked in the tenants' favor. This would be a particularly difficult path to follow.

Eviction notices were soon served. Our lawyer reminded us of the length of time this would take. On one particularly charged evening, as Michael and I struggled with how to express our divergent views, tears came. We were both on edge, and things weren't getting any better.

Just when I thought things would go further south with Michael, he said those words I had, subconsciously, longed to hear.

"Laura," he said, with a depth of meaning that I had not heard from him before. "We're in this together."

I didn't realize until I heard those words how important they were. They were even more precious than our "I love yous." When I heard them, I felt his full support of me. I felt lifted and strengthened.

We moved forward with greater ease from there. Soon, the townhouse was empty, and I placed her on the market for sale.

On closing day, I went to the townhouse to release her. Room by room, I thanked her. I thanked the guest room for serving my dad. I thanked the master bedroom for nurturing my dreams. In the kitchen, I appreciated the meals she helped provide. In the living room, my eyes teared up as I remembered the family laughter and joy we had shared there. I thanked the yard that had served as a play area for my puppies—and, lastly, I thanked the deck that had provided a space for sacred conversations, sacred self-care, and sacred growth.

I released her with a deep sense of gratitude for her service to my independent self.

Which brings me back to where I started: standing on the stoop after signing the deed, and officially releasing her to a wonderful young couple who would make her their first home together. I wondered which direction I should go in.

Had I made the right decision? It was an odd thought to have after all we had been through, and I wasn't sure how to deal with it.

As I drove home, I was overcome with emotion. Tears began; they came slowly at first, and then so fast and furiously that I had to pull over. These tears perplexed me. I had never felt any like them before. They were not grief tears. They were not happy tears.

I knew, from all the self-growth work that I have done, that I needed to be patient with them. I had to allow them, feel them, and release them to fully understand them. So I sat and cried on the side of the road, and when I'd finished, I drove to a nearby park and sat in contemplation.

"What was it that I was feeling so deeply inside?" I asked my soul. "What was it that I needed to understand?"

Then, the dark reality came. I realized what I had been avoiding for years. My soul sat patiently with me, waiting for me to understand, as I began to cry again. This time, the tears came because I had begun to hear my truth. These tears were of deep personal disappointment.

A deep truth was emerging about my relationship with Michael, and with myself. "It couldn't be that simple," I thought—and yet, it was. My heart ached deeply, but when the tears subsided, I was ready to hear the words of my soul.

My soul reminded me, "We are in this together."

My soul would always be my compass, and would guide me forward with the strength of the woman it knew.

And, at last, I knew what I had to do.

The townhouse had been my sanctuary—the place where the strong, independent woman within me had fully appeared. I had attached that part of me to the house, and had used her as a safety net as I stepped into my relationship with Michael, and with the next version of my best self. As long as she was there, I always had a safe place to retreat to if things didn't go as planned.

I arrived home to the house I shared with Michael, and walked in the door as if it was the first time. Michael was there. I cried. He laughed, not knowing the meaning of my tears. We hugged. I looked at him, knowing that, for so many years, I had been holding back from deeply connecting to him.

I looked at him and said, "We're in this together." And I knew, for the first time, the truest meaning of those words.

On that day, with gratitude, I released the townhouse. With grace, I stepped fully into being "in this together" with my life partner, and into the next version of my best self.

What does your home represent for you, and how do you identify with your home's meaning?

_____

_____

_____

_____

Do you have a "safety net" in your life? What is your relationship to it? How do you feel that it helps or hinders you in your life?

_____

_____

_____

_____

How might releasing your safety net enable you to step into something greater?

_____

_____

_____

_____

CHAPTER

Three

Grace is ...
Trusting The Process

Bombs Away!

Melissa Rapoport

I sat on the bench outside my shop, my face toward the sun, and watched my belongings trickle out the door.

"Sold," came the voice of the auctioneer through the open door.

A young couple, chatting animatedly, walked past, carrying my beloved espresso machine. They were followed by a parade of tables, chairs, espresso cups, saucers, and a shop full of restaurant equipment, all hustled out in the arms of restaurateurs looking for a good deal.

In a way, there was a strange sense of relief: maybe now the months of agonizing fighting could come to an end. But I also felt completely numb, as if suspended in air, watching but not feeling.

I hugged my sweater around my body, trying to make sense of what had led me to this day. I had heard the phrase, "You create your world"—but if that was true, how had I created the misery I was experiencing? It certainly wasn't *intentional*!

I thought back to earlier days, when my ex-husband and I were full of hope and pride at the community coffee shop we'd built from scratch. For twenty years, I saw the same people, day in and day out. I watched their lives change and grow. I watched them experience tragedy, and sometimes saw them find peace. I watched babies become college students, and middle-aged people become elderly.

There was Malcolm, who always sat on the bench with his cappuccino and toasted bagel with butter, playing guitar late into the summer afternoons. There was Emily, the dancer, who struggled in her relationship with her mother. There was Michael, who went through a divorce, then remarried the great love of his life and had a child with her. There were all the kids who hit milestones in my store: taking their first steps, using the toilet for the first time, and opening college acceptance letters that their parents brought from that day's mail.

With so much joy, and so many memories to build on, how did I now find myself in a legal dispute with my ex-husband and my new landlord? How was I carrying foreclosure papers on my new home? How had I created this world?

For most of my married life, I "went along." In order to be likable (or lovable, even), I just ... agreed. Experience had taught me that keeping the peace was better than dealing with the backlash of disagreement. I could deal with the yelling and arguing, but not the cold shoulder, the withdrawal of love. That punishment felt worse than just saying yes, because at least if I said yes he would still love me.

Beyond that (or maybe as an extension of that), I chose to be uninvolved in the financial aspects of our business, even post-divorce. At the time, I justified this by thinking I could not possibly do more than I was already doing. Acting as primary caregiver for our children and working in our stores was more than enough; I wanted to absolve myself from doing more. However, by not being involved in our finances, by not advocating for financial parity, I allowed others to determine my destiny. In essence, my finances happened *to* me rather than *by* me. I stunted my own ability to self-determine.

In our divorce process, I agreed to mediation—where my agreeableness played out in the usual way. I agreed and ignored to the tune of hundreds of thousands of dollars. I agreed and ignored to the point that I had to sell my home to stay afloat.

When I sold my home, I thought, *No more. It ends here, and I am going to reclaim what I've lost!*

Life as I knew it changed the day I decided to take a stand. It triggered a lawsuit between my ex-husband and me that had serious consequences. It cost both of us financially, ended our ability to run a business together, and (perhaps most importantly), created a situation that put undue stress on our children—a stressor that continues to play out for them to this day, as they navigate their own relationships with parents who no longer talk to one another.

For many years I lived in the aftermath of "my stand." The rubble engulfed me as I fought to rebuild a structure that no longer existed. Determined to keep my life as familiar as possible, I opened a new café just half a block from the one my ex-husband and I originally operated. Disaster was written on the walls before I signed the lease, but in my furious attempt to keep some semblance of sameness, I refused to see it.

Promises made by the landlord went unfulfilled. Nine months later, still without a storefront and with no protection written into my lease, I found myself once again in court.

Why does this keep happening to me? I wondered. *What am I doing wrong?*

"Ms. Rapoport," the auctioneer said, breaking my reverie. "We're finished."

I walked into my shop. It was empty, and that emptiness exposed the shattered dreams, the years of hard work now lost. I walked through the echoing room, running my hand over the honey-colored choppingblock counter where my regular customers had chatted with me. I took down the beautiful Kauai coffee bag in its shadowbox frame, and remembered with a faint smile my visit to the coffee plantation from which it had come.

Closing my café was the final detonation, the last *Ka-Boom* that forced me out from under the rubble that weighed me down. And, miraculously, as the mushroom cloud started to clear, I realized opportunity was in front of me.

The first thing I did was slow down.

The second thing I did was downsize.

The third thing I did was begin to breathe again.

It was in the magical space of slowing down that the image of rejuvenation started to develop. Seeds of growth were peeking through the rubble: the ground was fertile, the seedlings determined and able. Where before I'd wondered, "How did I create this misery?" I now contemplated, "What world shall I create for myself?"

I let the answers unfold. I started reading nutrition books, and began to understand that everything I put in my body was intimately connected to healing my Self. I eliminated sugar and processed food, and literally imagined the nutrients coursing through my body, feeding my ability to self-create. I could see the glow beginning to return to my skin and hair.

I began to take long walks in Central Park, taking in the green leaves, the swaths of soft grass, the scamper of small creatures as I walked through the woods. I sat on a small cliff overhanging a brook, listening to the water find its way through the rocks. The ebb and flow of nature, the ability of water to slip through the tiniest of places without dislodging its environment, the gradual change of the plants and leaves from one day to the next; these became symbolic of the way I wanted to live my life.

It became clear that I needed to welcome practices into my life that would strengthen my roots, that would allow me to grow with my face toward the sky, and that would nurture the unfurling of my own petals. I was ready to blossom, find my inner beauty, and find my truth.

I was ready to be alive.

I committed to my daily meditation practice, something that had become sporadic in the year leading up to the auction. I reached out to friends and apologized for being absent. I started exercising on a regular basis. I started to look for the opportunities being presented to me. I started saying, "Yes!"

Perhaps the biggest gift of this process was the opportunity to spend time with my teenage daughters, unhurried, unscheduled, without an agenda. We talked, we walked, we cooked. We spent a month together at the beach. Where I had always "made time" for them, having meals together, loving and nurturing them, this was different. I was *present*. Now, I could listen without simultaneously constructing an answer, hurrying them to make their point, or interrupting them because I did not have time. I let our time together unfold, and in that unfolding my love of them deepened into understanding and acceptance. I felt like the luckiest mom alive.

I now understand that my story is the uncovering of grace and gratitude. It was not a destination. It was not conscious. I did not wake up one day and think, "If I start a gratitude practice, my life will be better." Grace and gratitude was the unseen gift. It is the one deeply-seeded "way" that now drives every interaction with every person I encounter.

As I'm writing this, I'm sitting in the garden of my new home—a home I share with the love of my life. Physically and metaphorically, I am bringing back to life a garden long neglected. Rather than rushing to the nursery to fill the empty beds, I think about the plants that thrive in shade, the plants that require the unrelenting summer sun, and those that are adaptable to either. I scour gardening books to learn about plants that not only coexist, but are interdependent, and thrive in the presence of one another. My garden represents my rebirth: the rubble no longer ruins, but artifacts.

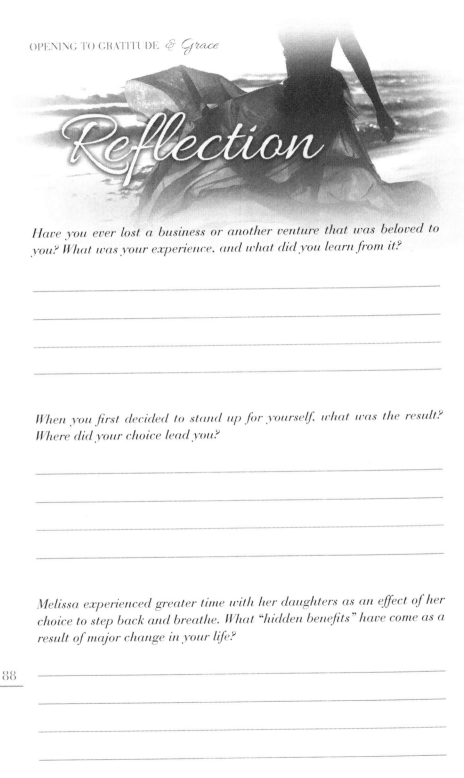

Reflection

Have you ever lost a business or another venture that was beloved to you? What was your experience, and what did you learn from it?

_____

_____

_____

_____

When you first decided to stand up for yourself, what was the result? Where did your choice lead you?

_____

_____

_____

_____

Melissa experienced greater time with her daughters as an effect of her choice to step back and breathe. What "hidden benefits" have come as a result of major change in your life?

_____

_____

_____

_____

Following Love

Sheila Callaham

I looked at my long list of to-dos and placed a check mark after each accomplished task. New roof: check. New garage doors: check. Refinish wood floors: check. Almost everything was done, and the remaining project—painting, inside and out—was already on the schedule.

I had wanted these dream projects completed for a long time. At last I would experience my home at its best—but not for long. These improvements were not meant for my enjoyment, but in preparation to sell the home I had fallen in love with the first moment I saw it.

It was more than twelve years ago when my husband Tom and I agreed to meet the realtor during our lunch break to visit the property which would, over time, become known as Dog Hill. As we drove to meet her, we asked ourselves why. After two years of searching, we had given up on finding the perfect house. Just a week before, we had refinanced our current home and signed a contract for a new addition. We shook our heads, embarrassed for wasting the realtor's time with our mid-day amusement.

The property sat on a hill at the end of a cul-de-sac, on a street thick with trees. The realtor was waiting at the bottom of the drive when we arrived, and we followed her up the steep hill to park. The home was brick front, transitional in style, with a huge picture window in the front. Tom and I got out and took in the view. The lot was private and heavily wooded. I was in heaven.

Inside, the home had everything we were looking for: five bedrooms for our large family, a combined living and dining room, and a walk-out basement with a library, playroom, and (much to our chagrin) an exercise room. At some point, Tom and I went our separate ways, privately taking in the house and grounds. When I think back on that day, I distinctly remember how enamored I was with it all. In my mind, I was already visualizing how beautiful my gardens would look.

When we finally headed back to work, we realized that our tour of the property had taken more than an hour.

A week later, we were under contract to purchase the home. When we closed on the new property several weeks after that, construction for the new addition had not yet begun on the home we were leaving behind. It was a financial risk, to be sure, but Tom and I felt so connected to our future home that we knew everything would work out. And of course, it did. Six weeks after moving to Dog Hill the addition was complete, and the house went on the market. It wasn't long until a sold sign went up—a confirmation that trusting our hearts had a better payoff than trusting our heads.

Yes, Dog Hill has been a wonderful home for all of us. Just ask any of our six kids, or the twelve rescued dogs who have called Dog Hill home.

So why leave?

I was following love.

Tom had been restless for the last several years, itching for a change. He spent hours online looking at homes, calling me over to check out the great locations or spectacular views his searches revealed. At first, when I looked at his property finds, the thought of leaving Dog Hill affected me so strongly that I felt sick to my stomach.

After a couple of years of my hubby's home searches, I became irritated. Didn't he realize that I had no intention of leaving? Still, he persisted. Washington. Florida. Texas. Timbuktu. Night after night, he searched for the perfect house while I sulked because he didn't realize we already had it.

I'm not sure when I caved, but Tom eventually convinced me to "just look" at a few homes during a family vacation in Florida. So I looked. Then he asked again during our next trip to Florida. I looked again. When we found an interesting house, Tom put in a bid. I held my breath that it wouldn't work out. It didn't.

A few months later, we decided to celebrate Tom's sixtieth birthday with a trip to Texas. I had only visited Texas once during a business trip to San Antonio, but Tom had lived in Austin for eight years and loved it. He had wanted us to make a trip to Texas for a long time; according to him, *everything* was bigger and better in Texas.

True to form, Tom spent months scouting out homes in the Hill Country that we could "look at" while we were there. When we boarded the plane heading west, we had agreed to see ten homes on the list, three of them starred as top picks. By the time we arrived, only two of the top picks remained.

Of those two, one would become ours.

It was a property that, much like Dog Hill, appealed to us by feel—so much so that, after we were under contract, we had to look at the pictures to remember how the house looked.

Back home, I began packing boxes with a heavy heart. I knew how excited Tom felt about moving back to Texas, and admittedly, the house was lovely. But it wasn't Dog Hill. With every box I taped closed, my heart ached even more at the thought of leaving.

It wasn't just Dog Hill itself that I mourned, it was the life we had built there. It was the thought of leaving our neighbors with whom we had developed friendships, the schools that had been so supportive of our children, and the community that was ... well, home!

A couple of weeks before the move, my neighbor asked if I had seen the albino deer. I said I had not, and he showed me a picture taken by a man down the road. I looked at the photo and admired the doe's beauty. I deeply longed to see such a sight, but the odds of that ever happening were against me more now than ever before, with the pending move.

Later that evening, I remembered the photo and thought about the elusive albino deer. I wondered where she slept at night, and which paths she walked. Most of all, I wondered why I had never seen her. At that moment, a little prayer went up. *Wouldn't it be nice*, I thought, *if I could see her just once before I go?*

The morning before our moving van departed Dog Hill for our cross-country adventure to Texas, I was upstairs packing yet another box when I heard Tom calling me.

"Quick!" he shouted. "You've got to see this!"

I sighed, annoyed by the interruption, and looked over the stair railing into the living room below where he sat upright, camera in hand, staring out the window.

"It's the albino deer!" he exclaimed.

I barreled down the stairs, pulling my phone from my pocket so I could take pictures. Cautiously approaching the window so as not to frighten her, I saw her standing on a well-worn deer path about thirty yards away. Warm tears blurred my vision, for I immediately knew this was the answer to my prayer. It was, in the language of the Universe, a parting gift, a confirmation that all would be well.

She stood on the path, looking ahead, ears erect as if she knew she was being admired for her rare beauty. Behind her stood several other deer, waiting to follow wherever she led. I was mesmerized. She turned away to pull at a low-hanging branch, and then raised her head once more, ears twitching in her vigilant stance. Finally, she lifted one front leg, paused … and, in a few leaps and bounds, she and her entourage crossed the driveway and disappeared onto the neighboring property.

I returned upstairs to cry—not tears of sadness, but tears of gratitude for the grace bestowed upon me, and for the assurance that leaving one home I loved didn't mean I couldn't come to love another one as much, or more.

And then it hit me. It wasn't *me* who'd spotted the albino deer. It was Tom who saw her and called to me. It was through him that I would have the chance to experience, again, what I so deeply longed for.

The next day, we began our journey: Tom ahead in the moving truck, and me following behind. I slowed the car to a stop at the deer trail where, just the morning before, nature had gifted me with the sighting of the beautiful albino doe. In my heart, I gave thanks, and brushed away a tear of gratitude that trailed down my cheek.

Then, satisfied, I released the brake, and we drove away. I was following love, and I knew it would not disappoint.

In what area of your life might you be resisting change?

_____

_____

_____

_____

How might you experience life differently if you were to let go of your current home and community?

_____

_____

_____

_____

Do you have a loving relationship that pushes you out of your comfort zone? How does that experience deepen your love?

_____

93

_____

_____

_____

All or Nothing

Stacey Curnow

*O*n a cold night in February 2011, I realized that I was trapped in a life that no longer fit.

I'd just received an e-mail from my manager saying that some of my midwifery colleagues at the hospital had a problem with me. I wasn't a "team player," they said, and now my manager was calling for a meeting to discuss the issue.

I was in shock. If you had asked me even a few days earlier if all was well at the hospital, I would have answered an unequivocal "Yes." Now, though, I wondered if I had been denying the signs, and that maybe all had *not* been well for a long time.

Even though I still loved some aspects of my job—providing quality health care to poor and under-served women—the job didn't make me come alive as it once had. Before, I used to fill my schedule with professional trainings and seminars, and welcomed opportunities to work extra shifts; now, I found other things much more compelling, like spending time with my young son or building my coaching practice. Still, I was grateful that my work was meaningful, and the income and benefits were good. Whenever I became aware of a negative thought, I quickly reminded myself, "It's not that bad."

And yet, it *had* gotten that bad, if my colleagues were complaining about me.

I tried to reassure myself that there was some misunderstanding, and that everything could easily be cleared up in the meeting, but I couldn't shake the feeling that something was very wrong.

I managed to fall asleep that night, but woke up a few hours later in a total panic. My heart was beating out of my chest, my body shaking and drenched in cold sweat. I cried out to God, the Universe, whoever would listen. "Why is this happening?"

The answer came, and it was very clear: *"You're not supposed to be here."*

I knew the voice didn't mean "here"—as in, here in my bed. It meant something much bigger and deeper—and I knew what that "something" was.

In June of 2009, while serving as a nurse-midwife in a busy public hospital birthing center (the aforementioned career to which I had devoted my entire adult life), I started my coaching business as a "side gig." I had realized that my favorite part of the day wasn't necessarily catching babies—although that was lovely—but talking with a woman during her pre- or postnatal visit about her hopes and dreams for her life, and the dramatic changes that were coming now that she was a mother.

One particularly memorable patient had a difficult birth, and her baby ended up needing care in the NICU for a few weeks before he was strong enough to go home. Before the birth, my patient had been sure she would go back to work after six weeks of maternity leave. Now that she had almost lost her son, she didn't want to go back at all—but as a single mom, she didn't know how she could afford *not* to. After we talked a long time about all of her options, she elected to leave her job and move to a different state and live with her sister and her sister's family. She would be a live-in nanny, and help care for her young niece and nephew as she cared for her own son.

I loved helping this woman visualize her dream and make it a reality, and wondered how I could do more of this work. I wanted to make these small parts of my day, for which I felt so profoundly grateful, the full focus of my professional life. When I realized that that's what life coaches do all day long, I felt like I finally had the vision of the life I was meant to live and what it would take to achieve it.

But there was a problem: I couldn't imagine giving up my hospital job. My husband Doug was an under-employed writer and didn't have health insurance. The steady income and all the other benefits of full employment were things I always provided for our family. Unlike my patient, I didn't see moving in with my extended family as an option, so how would we be able to survive without my salaried, benefitted position?

I felt that I had no choice but to maintain my hospital job while I built my coaching practice on the side. But the more excited I became about my business, the less enchanted I became with many aspects of my hospital job. The worst part was admitting the huge toll my twenty-four-hour shifts were taking on every part of my life—physical, mental, emotional, spiritual, and relational. I'd managed to bring my son, Griffin, to work with me from the time he was a newborn—he and Doug stayed in the tiny "call" room while I worked on the Labor and Delivery unit—but now that he was two, the administration, who'd never been happy about the arrangement, said I had to stop bringing him. We made the best of it, but something shifted: I was no longer willing to take on extra hours, because they would keep me away from my son.

That change—my refusal to do overtime—was, I realized, the main reason my colleagues didn't see me as a "team player." I refused to be flexible with my priorities.

My days as a staff midwife were numbered, and I knew it—but I still believed that our family needed the "security" my job provided. I *thought* my coaching business and writing career could support us, but I had no guarantees ... and my uncertainty led me right back around to wondering why I couldn't just be happy with my job at the hospital. Why couldn't I be a "team player"? It wasn't that bad, was it?

These stressful thoughts were what led to my panic attack on that dark February night. I couldn't believe I was in such a bad place: overwhelmed by doomsday scenarios of my uninsured family getting sick, of us losing our home and living in a van by the river, of me failing at my business and never finding another job as a midwife, because obstetrics is a very technical field and when you leave for even a short time the assumption is that you'll lose your skills and be unemployable ... I was in full-on breakdown mode.

But here's what I learned that day: a breakdown is always followed by a breakthrough. It's actually a Universal Law. We are never given a challenge unless the means of healing it *is right in front of us.*

Every time my dark fears arose, alongside them would come a moment of clarity when I *knew* I could give up my staff position. But then, the moment would pass, my heart would start racing again, and I'd break down in tears because I couldn't *possibly* leave. What saved me was that I couldn't make myself believe that I had been brought this far to fail.

Somewhere in the midst of thinking about everything I didn't want, a small voice inside me asked, "Okay, well, what *do* you want?"

I answered immediately. "I want both my husband and me to do work that's completely aligned with our life purpose. I want to do work I love, and be paid handsomely for it."

As soon as I got clear on what I really wanted, I received a gift in the form of a thought: *Only my own lack of gratitude and awareness of grace keeps me from living my dream life.* Saying an absolute "yes" to my dream life would bring me closer to it.

After that night, I dedicated myself to showing up for my life with a new, more profound sense of gratitude, and an absolute knowing that grace was manifesting itself in my life in surprising and miraculous ways every day. As I let go of my fears and the illusion of lack, I started to see more and more opportunities for growth and expansion. Doug and I agreed that if my business couldn't support our family, we would move to Guatemala, where we could live quite well on the rental income from our house. I started paying attention to the signs I received, and learned to *trust the path.*

My dream life didn't happen overnight, or that year. It was in April of 2014—more than three years after my midnight panic attack—that I confidently walked away from my twenty-year career as a nurse-midwife and into the unknown.

That night in 2011, I didn't decide to chuck it all and start over, but I did make an all-or-nothing decision: to stop wishing and hoping and making excuses, and instead do whatever it took to build a successful business that would support me and my family. Once I was no longer focusing my energy on what I didn't want, I was free to direct it toward what I *did* want.

I don't lament that it took me five years to achieve my dream. I thank God every day that I took that first shaky step back in 2009, which led to the all-out decision in 2011, which then led to the dream life I'm living today.

The secret to personal transformation, for me, was letting go of the illusion of control, and leaning into the gratitude and grace which is available to us in every moment. Those two practices—letting go and leaning in—were what led me to where I am today: fully present to the miracle of my life, and profoundly grateful that I get to live it.

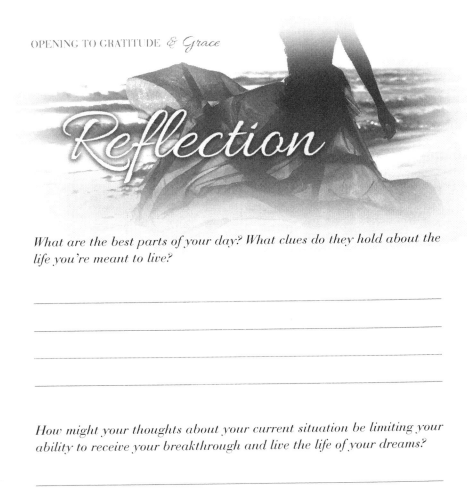

What are the best parts of your day? What clues do they hold about the life you're meant to live?

_____

_____

_____

_____

How might your thoughts about your current situation be limiting your ability to receive your breakthrough and live the life of your dreams?

_____

_____

_____

_____

How can you set yourself free by expressing gratitude and becoming more aware of the grace that is present in your life right now?

_____

_____

_____

_____

Time Will Pass

Pamela Henry

"*H*elp me!" I cried.

I was lying on the cold stone steps. Everything was spinning in slow motion. I was about to face the most terrifying experience of my life.

Only a couple of hours previously, my partner and I had arrived in the Turkish Riviera, excited to celebrate the marriage of old friends. The late-afternoon horizon clung softly to the blue coast. Our small bus hugged each perilous curve as we climbed the narrow mountain road. Forty minutes later, we arrived at the small, family-run resort where the wedding party was staying.

The excited chatter of wedding plans echoed in the stillness. Darkness fell as we enjoyed a light dinner under the open sky.

Before tucking in, I was asked to help move a case of wine into storage in preparation for the impending celebration. "It would be safer to put those in a box," my partner cautioned—but disregarding his fateful words, the bride-to-be and I loaded our arms with bottles and headed off toward our rooms.

I was exhausted from a day of travel, and didn't notice the unevenness of the worn stone staircase. I glanced up at the landing and thought, *We're almost there.*

In that instant, my shoe caught the edge of the next stair. Half a dozen wine bottles flew from my arms, and smashed into shards on the polished stone. Time stood still—and then, abruptly, my left arm crashed into the stone railing. I broke my fall with my right hand, which landed on the chunks of broken glass.

Gushing shades of crimson blended together on the stone stairs.

Terror coursed through my veins as searing pain shot through my left shoulder.

I lay there, frozen with shock, as the severity of my situation began to register with everyone around me. My girlfriend bound my hand to slow the bleeding, but the cut was too deep to treat at the resort. Somehow, I would have to face a forty-minute ride down the mountain to the hospital. My thoughts became hazy, fading in and out. I wondered if my time had come—if I would bleed to death there on the stairs.

I screamed inside as the doctor picked the remaining pieces of glass out of my hand. The disinfectant he poured over the open wound was even more excruciating. I couldn't take my eyes off the gaping red hole in my hand. How could this have happened?

The doctor crossed my wrists over my heart center to abate the bleeding, and securely strapped them in place. Then, he uttered the words that none of us were prepared to hear. "We can't perform your surgery here."

Surgery? *What?*

From that small emergency room in a seaside village, with only our passports and a credit card, my partner and I were ushered into an ambulance bound for the University Hospital in Antalya, four hours away.

I prayed for a miracle.

The painkillers hadn't kicked in. My thoughts reflected the hypnotic spin of the red ambulance light as it lit up the Turkish night. "Time will pass, time will pass," became my mantra.

What about the wedding? It was only three days away, and I was the Maid of Honor. What if I couldn't get back in time? How could I let my friend down like that?

We arrived at the hospital as morning broke. It was Ramadan, and everything was quiet and still. There wasn't an English-speaking person to be found. I was broken, scared, freezing beneath the light hospital gown—and I'd just realized that the index finger on my right hand wasn't bending.

Time will pass, time will pass ...

The hours felt like days as I was bounced from room to room. My panic grew. Wasn't there anyone who could translate the details of my injuries, and tell us what would happen next? My partner had made the difficult decision to leave me behind and venture into the city for essential supplies, so I was completely alone with my hazy thoughts. All I could do was surrender, and trust that my prayers were heard.

In the midafternoon, we learned that the hospital had an English-speaking liaison. My heart lightened when she told us that I was in the best hospital in the country for the surgery I required. My X-rays showed two severed tendons and a severed artery in my right hand, in addition to multiple fractures in my upper left arm.

Less than 24 hours after we arrived in Turkey, I was scheduled for microsurgery to repair my hand. Every cell of my being trembled in inexplicable fear as the attendants rolled my gurney down the long, austere hallway.

Time will pass, time will pass ... Was this really me, lying here? Past, present, and future mingled in a swirl of unrecognizable words as the doctors prepared for my surgery.

Amidst the blur, a face coalesced. The nurse leaned over me, looked into my eyes, and in soft, crystal-clear English, spoke the words that changed everything.

"You're going to be okay. Everything is fine." Her compassionate smile infused me with peace. Sweet relief washed over me, and I knew all was well.

Then, she vanished.

In the years since my surgery, I've often reflected on this profound moment. At first, I wondered who she was, and wished that I could share my gratitude for her gift of grace. Then, I learned that, in extenuating circumstances, guardian angels have been known to appear in physical form. With that revelation, the same sense of peace that I'd felt in the operating room washed over me. I knew, then, that it had been her: my angel.

After the operation, I woke up in my room to find my very relieved partner sitting beside me. The surgery had been a success, and we still had forty-eight hours before the wedding started.

Although the next few days were critical to my healing, all I cared about was making it back in time to stand beside my friend as she said, "I do." My doctor was reluctant to let me go, but I prayed for release.

My prayer was answered, but not without jumping another hurdle.

On the day of the wedding, just as we were preparing to leave, we discovered that the hospital needed to hold my passport until my insurance confirmation could be located. That wasn't likely to happen until after the weekend.

Now what? We had already missed the wedding ceremony.

Taking a leap of faith, we left the hospital and my passport behind. By the time we arrived at the resort, the wedding reception was in full swing. I was so grateful to witness my friend's joy, it felt like eons since I had taken my near-fatal step.

As the evening festivities came to a close, the wedding party traveled back down the mountain and boarded two sailboats for a four-day cruise along the blue Turkish coast.

I spent those days gazing out across the azure water, contemplating what had happened. Both of my arms were bound to prevent my sutures from splitting and my shoulder from becoming misaligned, so there wasn't much else I *could* do. In spite of my frustration, I felt deeply grateful for the loving support that surrounded me.

Although I couldn't see it at the time, my adventure offered wisdom that would eventually open me to receiving a greater understanding of gratitude and grace.

Gratitude is a state of being. It teaches us to be here and now, grounded in the awareness of our surroundings, without dwelling in the past or projecting into the future. Had I been present when I filled my arms with wine bottles, I would have heeded my partner's fateful words and perhaps avoided a near-fatal situation.

Grace holds the key to who we truly are. We are infinitely supported, and this gift of Spirit is the essence of a greater power within us, even when we are not consciously aware of it. As I lay on that operating table, the gift of grace transformed my experience as my guardian angel lifted my burden of fear.

Gratitude and grace merge in the ebb and flow of surrender. When we release the perceived notion that we are in control, we fall into the unconditional arms of boundless love, support, and well-being.

As for my personal mantra, "Time will pass" has evolved into "I am here, now." It reminds me that gratitude and grace flow from presence:

Presence of mind.
Presence of body.
Presence of spirit.
I am here, now.

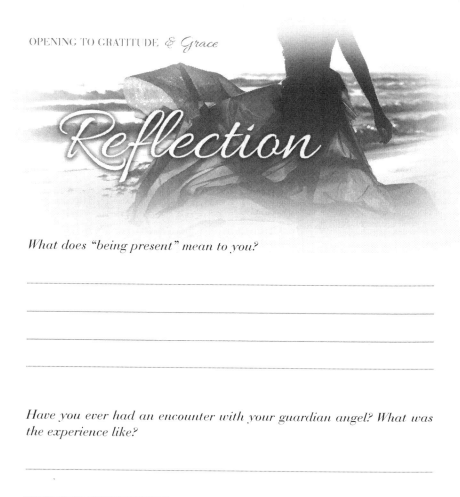

Reflection

What does "being present" mean to you?

Have you ever had an encounter with your guardian angel? What was the experience like?

Pamela writes, "Gratitude and grace merge in the ebb and flow of surrender." Where in your life can you surrender to grace? What would it look like to let go of control?

How My Divorce Saved My Life

Stacey Murphy

January 15, 1999, was my Independence Day—the day I took my life back.

I remember it clearly. I was lying on my green sofa with tears in my eyes. My body was riddled with pain, my heart was heavy, and life was whipping me around like a rag doll. I turned to my husband and said, "I can no longer live this life. I'm leaving."

My daughter, the precious baby I'd wanted so badly, was eighteen months old, and this time of nurturing her precious little soul should have been the best of my life. But instead of feeling joyful, I was depressed, angry, and frustrated—and my negative emotions were keeping me locked in the jaws of illness.

After my daughter's birth, my health took a drastic turn for the worst. I had just been diagnosed with fibromyalgia, and was simultaneously suffering from shingles and walking pneumonia. My doctor was growing steadily more concerned. Finally, he uttered the words that would change my life.

"You're young," he said, "but your body is shutting down. Whatever is stressing you out, you need to get a handle on it, because you're slowly killing yourself."

Shock and horror overcame me. I thought, *I'm too young to die!* I had just brought a precious life into the world, but I was letting my own life slip away.

I went home with the doctor's words echoing in my brain. *Killing yourself. You're killing yourself. You're killing yourself ...* How had my life turned into this sorry tale?

Back at home, I looked in the mirror, but didn't recognize the woman looking back at me. Instead, I saw a shell of a person, a prototype of the woman everyone thought I should be. All my life, I'd focused on gaining outside approval and validation. I believed that if I achieved great things, I would finally be offered the love and acceptance I hadn't felt growing up. My Catholic guilt went deep, and I was still holding onto the shame of Original Sin, believing I was flawed but that success would prove my worthiness. But, as I was discovering, the path I'd been told would ensure my security and happiness—college degree, Fortune 500 career, marriage, and a child—hadn't done so. I'd just carried those feelings of self-loathing and self-hatred forward into my marriage and career. Instead of doing what my parents expected of me, now I did what my husband expected of me, and stuffed my feelings deep into my body.

Guilt, fear, and shame had ruled me since childhood—and now, they were killing me.

Standing in front of that mirror, I saw what a lifetime of low self-worth and lack of self-confidence had created. Tears of anger and frustration at myself surfaced, but they were quickly overruled.

"I want to live," I told my reflection. "I want to be there for my daughter, and I want to be happy."

In that moment, I decided to take a stand for *me*, before it was too late.

I needed to learn to love myself—all of me, even the parts I'd been told were bad or wrong. More importantly, I needed to learn to be a healthy and loving role model for my daughter. Even though my body didn't feel strong, my heart and mind were ready to fight.

Acting on faith, I ended my suffocating marriage, with all of its expectations. For the first time in my life, I was able to take off my mask, and experience what true living felt like.

108

I was like a thirsty woman in the Sahara Desert, soaking up all the spiritual knowledge I could get my hands on. I wanted to *live*, damn it! I wanted my inner child to finally feel unconditional love, and heal the deep wounds of guilt, shame, and fear she'd suffered with for so long. I couldn't get enough; I desired a true transformation.

My journey led me to a weekend spiritual retreat. I was excited to see the many spiritual teachers who were my Earth Angels. The hotel was buzzing with other spiritual warriors; we were like kids in a candy store. I attended as many workshops as my schedule would fit—but there was one expert who radically changed the direction of my path and life purpose.

Her name was Margot Anand, and she was an internationally acclaimed Tantra teacher. At the time, she was in her fifties. Casual, understated in her dress, she strutted barefoot across the stage. With her French accent, she spoke about the pleasures of life: vibrant health, a fulfilling business … and her desire for and love of sex!

As she shared her wisdom, she caressed her body with a beaming smile on her face. She made these yummy sounds on stage in front of three hundred people. Joy and radiance emanated from her as she spoke about the importance of infusing your life with pleasure.

I said to myself, "I want some of that!"

That was the start of my journey into the sensual and seductive arts. I had found the missing piece in my life. For too long, I didn't experience pleasure. From my Catholic upbringing, I'd learned that pleasures of the body were to be denied, not embraced. Being able to embrace life's pleasures without guilt or shame was *so* foreign to me. But the door to my cage was cracked, and as I greeted the new millennium I allowed my mind to fly free of restriction.

It took eight more years—but at last, my cage was busted wide open.

I asked the Universe to provide me with clarity concerning my life's purpose. I was loving my life more than ever, but I knew I was meant for more than corporate America. I was itching to make a difference in the world, and help others heal their lives as I had done. It took the Universe no time at all to answer my call. Within weeks, it hit me in one simple word.

Tantra.

The voice of the Universe woke me out of my sleep. I heard the word clear as day. I looked around to see if someone else was in the room with me … but no, it was just me.

Dumbfounded, I asked, "Why Tantra? Why sex?"

Tantra teaches the beautiful synergy of spiritual and sexual energies, and how we can integrate all parts of ourselves in a divine experience. But sex was (and still is) a touchy subject in our society. I had no idea what do to with this, so I lamented to a friend.

"You asked a question, and the Universe answered," she told me.

"Yes, but why *me?*"

"Why *not* you?" she countered.

If I was going to move forward, I needed to have unwavering faith in myself and the universe. So I stepped into Tantra, and I never looked back.

My Tantric studies led me to teach basic erotic education to women. I was captivated by the look of hope on my students' faces. These women wanted to know how to make their love and sex lives better—and it was witnessing this desire that led me to become a Certified Sex Coach. I pushed past the old fears of "what will people think?" that had kept me captive for so long, and decided to play big in the world by accepting my purpose with gratitude and grace.

The greatest gift we have to give is often the very thing we need to heal. Today, I'm happily liberated from corporate America and following my own path. Not only am I in an amazing relationship, I'm a full-time Certified Intimacy Coach. Known as the Queen of Juicy Love, I receive great pleasure in helping women reclaim their sensual joy, seductive essence, and self-confidence so that, like me, they can move from toxic love to relationship bliss.

At the end of the day, we all want to feel empowered, desirable, and happy—and I'm helping women create that for themselves.

If I had chosen to remain a victim, I don't know if I would still be alive. I'm forever grateful that I chose to trust myself, and step forward into my juicy life with grace.

How do the physical symptoms of stress, shame, and grief show up in your body? What steps can you take, right now, to heal them?

_____

_____

_____

_____

Stacey stepped past her shame to embrace the pleasures of life. Where can you open up to receive more pleasure in your own life?

_____

_____

_____

Often, our life's work can be found in our biggest lessons. How do your greatest lessons tie into your purpose?

_____

111

_____

_____

_____

Steamrolling Grace

Stacey Martino

*O*h my God, I thought to myself. *There are freakin' 2,800 people waiting to go into this room.*

Immediately, my wheels started turning.

You know how you can think three minutes' worth of thoughts in four seconds? Yeah, that's what happened next. If you'd been able to listen to my rapid-fire thoughts, they would have sounded something like this:

Okay. If I want that front row seat, I'm going to go through this door here (I think that's the one they opened first yesterday). Then, instead of running down the middle aisle, like most people, I'm going to go running through the seats to the right-side aisle and sail up to the front and over to the middle! I'll be in that front row—and I'll grab a seat for my buddy too, because if I wait for her I'll miss out on the seat I want. Besides, if I explain this to her it will take too much time. She might think I'm crazy. Can't have that. This is a big day. It's gonna be the best day! I've totally got this!

The doors opened, and I took off like a racehorse out of the gate!

I flew past people who were hugging and greeting each other with big smiles and a hearty "Good Morning!" I smiled at them, but on the inside I was thinking, *You will never get that front row seat with your hugs and your smiles! Watch me nail this!*

Bam! Bag down, water bottle down. Front row seats saved for me and my buddy. *That is how it is done, people!*

Now, I could hug. Now, I could dance. Now I could smile!

My nickname was "The Ice Princess." I was an over-achiever; a no-nonsense, get-it-done girl. But not to my man. Not to Paul. With

Paul, I was a totally different woman—his sunshine. Happiness, vulnerability, bliss, love, surrender, openness, passion … It was all there within me, but only for him.

He was there in the room, too, somewhere. I searched 2,800 faces looking for him. Last time I'd seen him was early that morning when we'd been assigned to our respective teams for the day's events.

I stood on a chair and scanned the crowd. Sure enough, I saw him—and what was he doing? Already locking his eyes on me. From the front row on the other side of the room, he threw a powerful fist in the air, as if to say, "I'm ready to rock this day!"

I wasn't surprised to see him in the front, even though I knew that he hadn't gone through any of the crazy shit I did to manipulate his way there. That's just Paul: he decides he's going to be in the front, and then he's just *there*. It just works out for him. He's so confident about it; he doesn't stress, he doesn't push, he just *is*.

Lucky bastard. I love that man!

Hours later, my world was transforming. The front row was definitely the right place for me to be for this personal development immersion. The next hour was going to change my life.

We were going through an exercise to figure out the repetitive thought patterns that were shaping our lives—and I was struggling big time. *What is mine?* I asked myself, panicking. *I have to know!*

I could sense how much time had passed, and my thoughts kept running. *I need to know this piece to get the most out of the next segment. Everybody else is going to go in with theirs, and I'm not going to know mine. I'm going to miss out on what I need most. I've gotta figure this out.*

I scribbled down notes, question after question. All of them resonated with me.

"If you're struggling to figure out which repetitive question is yours," the event leader began—

I'm listening!

" … Look at the questions you think might be yours. Have you asked yourself any of those in the last five minutes?"

The answer hit me like a ton of bricks.

Five minutes ago: *How am I going to figure out my question, so that I don't miss out on what I need the most?*

Hours ago: *How am I going to get the front row, so I don't miss out on the best day possible?*

Over and over and over, every day, for my whole life: *How can I control this?*

Tears streamed down my face. I took a deep breath, and said aloud: "This ends today."

That was eight years ago. Since then, I've learned that control is the opposite of faith, because "faith" means "trust." And as I began to cultivate my ability to remain open and trust, I learned to be grateful at all times and see the grace in every circumstance. I learned to differentiate between what was my work (to master myself) and what was God's work (everything else).

Last week, I attended a Mastermind meeting with our mentor to strategize about our business growth.

I was exhausted going into the meeting. I'd just come out of our major launch for the year, and this meant our business needed to grow to the next level to serve all of our new students and clients. And so, when my mentor looked me in the eye and said, "Stacey, it's time to add a Student Enrollment person to your team," my immediate answer was "No! Please don't add anything else to my to-do list right now!"

I knew that I needed someone to take over the conversations with people who wanted to become students, because I no longer had time to do it. But the thought of finding a new person, onboarding them, teaching them about all of our programs and events, introducing them to our culture, systems, and processes, and shadowing and supporting them ... No way! I needed to do less, not more!

But I began to feel uncomfortable, deep inside, because I knew my mentor was right. I just didn't know how to move forward with the time, energy, and resources I had at that moment.

My mentor reassured me. "You can do this, Stacey. There are people waiting for your help, and this is the next step."

I reminded myself to release control and trust. *God,* I thought, *I promise to take this step in service to the people you send me. Please*

help me do this.

Later, I wrote in my journal, *"Find a Student Enrollment Advocate, God will provide the 'how.'"*

That night at dinner, I told Paul everything that had happened. He smiled at me, and with his rock-solid confidence, said "It's Carol! You are describing Carol. She's already on our team and she's exactly the person we need."

My mind was racing. Carol already knew our programs and events, and understood our mission. She lived and breathed our culture, and was amazing with our students. She didn't need me to train or shadow her—she was ready to go!

I had been so resistant to the idea that I hadn't seen the solution.

On Monday, I explained the new developments to Carol and asked, "How would you feel about filling this role for us?"

I was floored by her response. She practically screamed with delight. "Stacey, last week, while you were at the Mastermind, I told my husband, 'I'm sensing that they are going to tell Stacey it's time to bring on an enrollment team to do phone calls and offer guidance to new students. How can I tell Stacey that I really want to be the one to serve our students in this role?'"

Tears of relief and gratitude came to my eyes. Once again, God had orchestrated all of the details for me!

If I had stayed in fear after that Mastermind session and said, "No, I'm really too busy," or, "Not right now, but maybe later we can look at that," then I never would have seen any of the grace. Everything was divinely arranged for me. Before I had even asked, it was given.

I spent the first half of my life controlling, pushing, driving, and making things look the way I thought they should. I was steamrolling grace! I'm quite sure that looking back, there were thousands of moments where grace had already delivered what I needed, but because I was controlling and pushing, I rolled right past it, never seeing it.

Through control and brute force, I got my outcome every time, but I missed out on what I call "The Bigger." The bigger outcome.

The dream you can't achieve through driving or pushing, because it's greater than what you can imagine for yourself.

God has bigger dreams for us than we do for ourselves. My work is to grow in self-mastery and how I relate to others, live in gratitude, and surrender to grace. God does all of the rest—and I get to delight in the thrill of living a life co-created with God!

It took me twenty-five years to learn that lesson, and another twenty to master it to the level I practice today—and I'm still learning and growing! It is my hope that your journey to enjoying a life of grace and ease will be much shorter than mine, but equally as blissful.

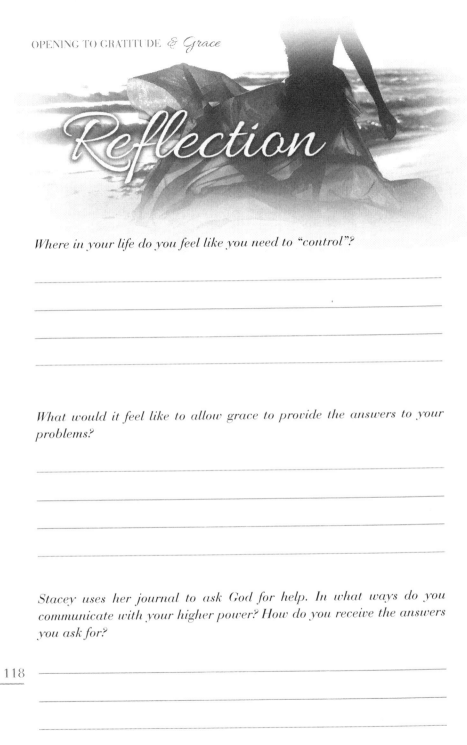

Reflection

Where in your life do you feel like you need to "control"?

_____

_____

_____

_____

What would it feel like to allow grace to provide the answers to your problems?

_____

_____

_____

_____

Stacey uses her journal to ask God for help. In what ways do you communicate with your higher power? How do you receive the answers you ask for?

118

_____

_____

_____

_____

CHAPTER
Four

Grace is ...
Our Heritage

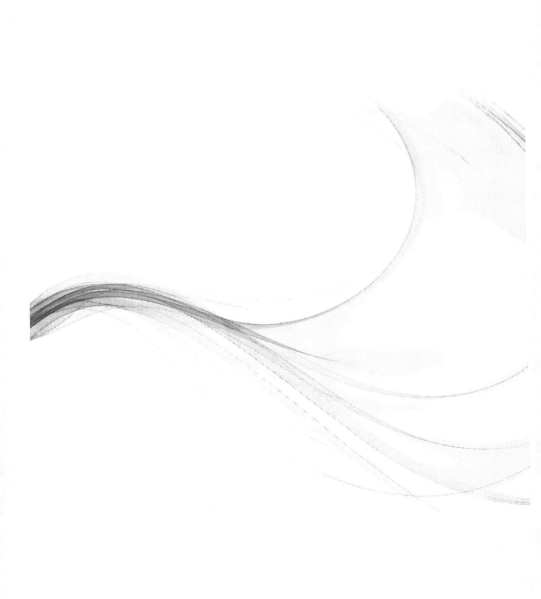

The Gray Suit

Jill Celeste, MA

I fumbled with the lock. My hands shook. I squelched my rising frustration and gave it another go. Finally, the lock turned, and I rolled back the storage unit door. It echoed throughout the hallway.

I stood back and gazed inside.

Here was everything my parents owned. Fifty-four years of furniture, appliances, paperwork, pictures, clothes, and memories stared back at me.

I choked back a sob. I had work to do. I was on a deadline.

Only months before, my husband, sons and I packed up my parents' apartment. We hurried through it all. There was no time for sorting, cleaning, or discarding. Everything just went into the nearest box.

I was on a deadline back then too, with no time for crying.

Six months ago, my mother showed up at my doorstep in tears. My father was living in a nursing home, and out of loneliness and despair, Mom hired the husband of her former cleaning lady to be her live-in care provider. In only a few months' time, he drained her savings account to pay for his probation fees, took over her car, forced the apartment complex to ask my mom to move out, and caused a wedge in our family that we may never bounce back from. He was a sociopath and a parasite.

On that August evening, Mom, knowing that this situation was not right, came to us for refuge, and we took her in.

We had one weekend to get everything out of her two-bedroom apartment. The parasite was still there. We worked around him as we piled everything into the moving truck.

When the last item was moved into the storage unit, I closed the door and walked away. I knew I was walking away from the good and bad memories, and avoiding my emotions, but I needed a break.

Fast-forward six months, and it was time to face the storage unit again. Mom, who had lived with us since that August evening, had just moved into an assisted living facility. My parents no longer needed ninety-nine percent of their belongings. It was time to sort, clean, and discard.

Before I drove to the storage unit facility that day, I made a game plan. Take pictures of the washer and dryer so we can post them on Craigslist. Get the microwave and convection oven in the car. Look for easy-to-grab items that I could drop off at the Goodwill trailer on my way home.

The washer and dryer stood at the front of the storage unit. I snapped some photos with my iPhone. I then looked for the microwave and convection oven. My husband created a small path around my parents' belongings, and I could see the appliances in the back. I loaded the microwave and convection oven onto the dolly.

So far, so good.

I was ready for the third step: looking for items for Goodwill. I stepped out of the storage unit and scanned the boxes, furniture, and loose items. The stray items caught my eye; they were perfect for donating.

I grabbed lamps, mops, blankets, and duffel bags. I was on a roll. I filled the dolly, but knew I had room for one more item.

Draped over a box was an old garment bag. Perfect! My parents would never need that garment bag again, and it would fit on the dolly and in my SUV. I pulled it down from its perch and was surprised how heavy it felt. I laid it over the washing machine and unzipped it, thinking Mom had stashed a blanket in there.

Only it wasn't a blanket. It was my father's gray suit, complete with a still-knotted blue tie.

My fingers rested on Dad's suit, and, before I could stop them, tears fell from my eyes like raindrops down a window pane.

Dad had worn this suit and tie at my wedding seventeen years before. Afterward, he'd placed it in the garment bag to keep it clean. My father would never wear this suit again. He wouldn't have a reason to. He couldn't even fit into it anymore. Months of advanced Alzheimer's disease had robbed him of his athletic physique, and he was wilting away in his bed in the nursing home.

I sat down on a small chair near the front of the storage unit, and stared at my father's suit, draped there over the washing machine. I'd tried so hard to push through my "assignments" and not give in to my emotions. All of this—the sorting, donating, and selling of my parents' belongings, the discarding of unwanted items—was something I wanted to get over with. It was painful. All I wanted was to rip off the proverbial Band-Aid, and having to stop for my emotions slowed me down.

I realized, though, as I sat staring at the gray suit, that I was making this process *more painful* because I was not allowing myself to feel the emotions: to cry, to remember, to grin, to be angry and sad. Furthermore, I was not allowing myself to feel gratitude.

Yes, the physical work of cleaning out a crammed-full storage unit was an arduous task. Sure, the emotional aspect was even more taxing. But I had so much to be thankful for!

I was raised by two parents who loved me with every fiber of their beings. I got to spend meaningful time with them for almost forty-three years before Alzheimer's took the best parts of my dad's brain. I was able to take care of my mom for six months, and keep her safe. And now, I had this opportunity to go through their belongings and reminisce about our wonderful lives together.

How blessed I am, I thought.

I stood up from the chair, laid a loving hand on my dad's suit, and removed it from the garment bag. I wasn't ready to part with the suit just yet, but I added the garment bag to the dolly. I rolled the storage unit door down and locked it. It was time to continue on with my tasks. Every weekend for almost two months, I returned to my parents' storage unit to do more sorting, cleaning, and discarding. Instead of dreading the task, though, I approached it with intense gratitude. I opened each box and allowed the emotions to flow. Sometimes the tears came—but more often, I found myself smiling as I remembered a family vacation, or a Christmas spent together.

How lucky I was to be the steward of my parents' belongings. How grateful I was to touch things *one more time* before deciding what to do with them. How gratifying it was to find new homes for many of their things.

John F. Kennedy once said: "We must find time to stop and thank the people who make a difference in our lives." With each box I opened, I did exactly that: I stopped and thanked. My soul swelled with gratitude as I held each item that once belonged to my parents. I sorted, cleaned, and discarded not just my parents' things, but my emotions too. I allowed myself to journey through the process of saying good-bye. Sure, I still felt sad, angry, and even hateful over what had happened, but slowly, positive emotions began to overshadow the negative.

Whenever I felt negative emotions creeping up, I would say, "*How blessed I was. How blessed I am.*" This mantra, as simple as it is, kept me in a grateful mindset. I continue to use it today whenever I am faced with a painful experience—which is often, as I cope with my parents' aging and final transitions. When I say those words, it staves off the negative feelings, and leaves me with two of the best: grace and gratitude. It is through that grace and gratitude that I handle life's many curveballs.

How blessed I was.

How blessed I am.

Do you ignore your emotions while completing a painful task? What would happen if you made room for your emotions during the process?

_____

_____

_____

_____

Do you have a tool, like Jill's mantra, that you use to shift negative emotions when they arise?

_____

_____

_____

_____

When was the last time you allowed yourself to be grateful for the elders in your life? How can you express this gratitude?

_____

125

_____

_____

_____

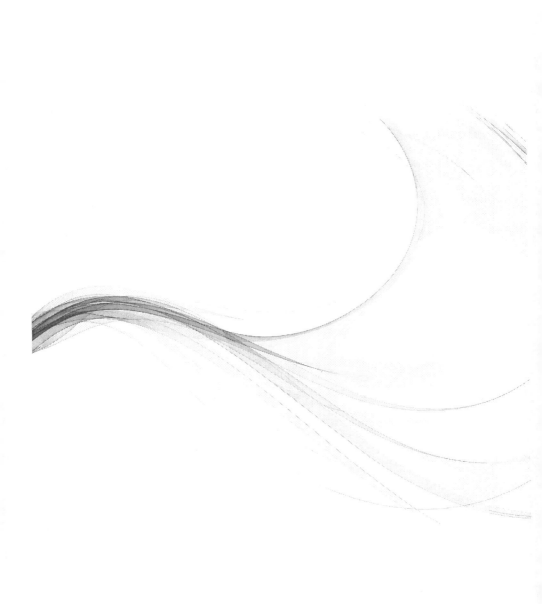

From the Seeds of Winter's Darkness

Kailean Welsh, MS, LPC

*I*t was a long, heavy winter. I felt engulfed in gray as the bleakness of Wisconsin in February surrounded me. Laid off from my job two weeks before Christmas, I was struggling to figure out what was next. Opportunities for a psychotherapist in my small hometown were nearly non-existent.

"Maybe it's time to start my own practice," I thought.

That idea had dawned years before in graduate school, when I envisioned a blending of psychotherapy and spirituality, and the positive impact I could have on people's lives working in such a way. Over the years, the dream had faded, a victim of the harsh realities of managed care, insurance, and needing to pay the bills.

Now, though, a glimmer of hope stirred as the seed of that earlier vision emerged through the depths of winter's darkness. Maybe, just maybe ...

I knew nothing about managing a business, so I signed up for a workshop with SCORE, a group of retired professionals who share their time and expertise to help entrepreneurs. The workshop was scheduled for the next day.

"Hi, Mom," I answered the phone, seeing my parents' number on the caller ID. It was always Mom who called. To my surprise, I heard Dad's voice.

Never one to beat around the bush, Dad got straight to the point. "I'm not going back to dialysis," he said. "Today was my last day."

Dad's eighty-one-year-old body was not working very well. He'd experienced some health issues that damaged his kidneys, and had been on dialysis three times a week for several months.

I hadn't known of his plan to try dialysis for only six months. If he wasn't feeling better by then, he'd decided, he wouldn't continue.

The six months were up.

"What does this mean?" I asked, knowing but not wanting to acknowledge the answer.

"I'm not really sure," he replied. "I'll have some time–a week, maybe a little more."

"I love you so much, Dad," was all I could say; tears made it hard to speak. "I'll come over."

"Not tonight. I have more calls to make. I know you have that program tomorrow. Go to that, and come by after."

Dad was a farmer, like his father before him. He lived by nature and the land. He was self-reliant and independent, so I had been surprised a few weeks earlier when he encouraged me to look for another agency position. He wanted me to have a regular schedule and a consistent paycheck, he said. He didn't want me to struggle.

Now, work seemed so inconsequential. I couldn't focus. All I could think about was Dad.

A man of strong faith, Dad was raised Catholic, and church had been an important part of his life. I had strayed from the church, but felt a deep spiritual hunger and had explored several faith traditions. Dad and I had many great conversations over the years about God and religion and the meaning of life.

Our relationship had not always been easy: Dad was stubborn, opinionated, and not the best listener. I felt small in the shadow of his powerful presence.

Dad and Mom built their life together on the farm. Originally, they worked the land the way everyone did, with the concept that more was better. They looked for more acres, raised more animals, and used more and more chemicals on the fields in the quest for higher yields.

That changed abruptly the day Dad's prized Angus cows were poisoned. In a single, heart-wrenching day, forty-four cows and calves became crazed and ill. Twenty of them died. Their deaths were attributed to the residue left on an empty insecticide bag that had tainted a large hay bale. Seeing the destructive power of this minimal trace of a product that was routinely spread on fields by the pounds, Dad decided he would never again put chemicals on his soil.

In a bold move, Dad left conventional farming methods behind. He became a pioneer in the organic movement, leading the way to a method of farming and food production that was effective, healthy, and sustainable. He committed to farming in a way that demonstrated a caring for all life.

It wasn't easy, especially at first. He was often a lone voice. There were difficulties and setbacks. People told him he'd never make it without using chemicals. They said he was foolish, an idealist.

Yet, Dad stayed true to his vision. It became his sacred task.

These thoughts swirled in my head as I sat in the SCORE workshop that day, considering my future as I pondered my dad's past.

Afterward, I drove the forty miles to my parents' home, feeling hesitant and unsure. My heart ached. I was eager to be with my dad, yet fearful of the days ahead. Many questions filled my mind; none had easy answers.

Several cars were parked outside when I arrived, a sign that the family was gathering. It was a harsh reminder of the reality of the situation. The living room was full. Dad was sitting in his recliner, one leg tucked under him, the other dangling over the armrest. Talking and smiling, he looked like a young child eagerly telling a story.

That set the tone for the upcoming days.

As word spread of Dad's decision, a steady stream of visitors came by. Dad continued to tell stories, sharing his memories, his joys, and his sorrows—all expressing his intense gratitude for a full life. The interactions were heartfelt and genuine. There was no time to hold back. People told Dad how they felt about him, what they appreciated about him, and how he'd touched their lives. He did the same in return. Together, we laughed and we cried. We celebrated Dad's life, and we prepared for his death.

It came gently.

Ten days later, on Wednesday, February 24, the hospice nurse alerted us that the end would come soon. Though still alert and engaged, Dad was sleeping more and clearly becoming weaker. We

129

gathered around his bed that evening, praying and singing, quietly sharing our limited time together.

"Would you sing 'One Tin Soldier'?" Dad asked.

My sister scurried off to the computer, and returned with several copies of the lyrics. Hesitantly, and a bit off-pitch, we brought voice to the words:

Listen, children, to a story that was written long ago,
About a kingdom on a mountain, and the valley-folk below.
On the mountain was a treasure, buried deep beneath the stone,
And the valley-people swore they'd have it for their very own ...

Dad lay on the bed, eyes closed, as we sang through the verses. The words revealed that the treasure sought and fought over was not gold or material riches. The coveted prize was simply peace on Earth.

I think that's why Dad so loved that song. It expressed for him what really mattered. It wasn't wealth or power, but love and peace and stewardship. It was living by a code of honor and doing what was his to do.

And, as the song concludes: *"One tin soldier rides away."*

Dad knew the next step in his journey was his alone. He sent us all to bed. My mom lay down beside him as she had every night for nearly sixty years—and as she drifted off to sleep next to him, their bodies breathing in unison, he died.

I opened my holistic psychotherapy practice a few months later. It wasn't easy, especially in the beginning. I heard the same comments that Dad had: "You're an idealist. You're never going to make it." I was scared, but I persisted. Like Dad, I felt driven to do what I felt was right. Returning psychotherapy to its roots as "care of the soul" became my sacred task. And, like Dad, despite the struggle, by following my passion I connected with a place deep inside and found great joy.

I think of Dad often. He lives on in me as I do my best to embody the characteristics I admired in him. He taught me courage, the importance of speaking my truth, contributing to the world, living in faith, and doing what is mine to do.

In life and at his death, Dad showed the way. With love, gratitude, and divine trust, through the darkest days of his own final winter, he led his family to holy ground. There he found the greatest treasure: the deep, abiding, peace of God's healing grace.

> *The state of grace needs the recipient in order to be complete.*
> *You are held in the hand of God and totally loved.*
> *And when that love can be received, the circuit is completed.*
>
> ~Emmanuel

What difficult experiences have moved you to make choices that you may not have made otherwise?

_____

_____

_____

_____

Kailean and her dad felt compelled to "do what is mine to do." Is there something that you feel driven to do, but have not yet taken action on? What is holding you back?

_____

_____

_____

_____

Is there someone in your family or inner circle who has taught you important life lessons? How do you express your gratitude for this person?

132

_____

_____

_____

_____

My First Spiritual Mentor

Shelley Riutta, MSE, LPC

*M*y mom called to me from the back porch. "Shelley, it's time to come in!"

I was seven years old. It was an overcast spring day, and I was playing on the grass with my Barbie dolls and my Barbie airplane. I packed up my toys, and headed for my bedroom to put everything away. My mom came in and sat down on the bed.

"Shelley, I have something I need to talk to you about. Your Grandma passed away, so you won't be able to see her anymore."

I couldn't quite comprehend what that meant, but a deep feeling of pain washed over my body. I quickly stuffed the pain deep inside; I knew that there wouldn't be support for those feelings in my home.

My grandmother was my first spiritual mentor, the one who guided me to connect more deeply with myself and the divine.

I remember sitting on the shores of Lake Superior with her as a young child. In silence, we watched the powerful waves crash onto the shore as the wind blew through our hair. I felt her loving and nurturing spirit. In those moments, I not only felt connected to her, but to myself, and to God.

I remember visiting my grandparents at their cottage in Upper Michigan. We would leave our house when my dad was done with work, and drive into the night. When I awoke in the morning, the sun would be sparkling across the lake, and I would feel so happy to be there with Grandma.

One night, when all the parents went out for dinner, my brother and I stayed behind at the cottage with Grandma. We slept in bed with her, one of us tucked under each of her arms. Late that night, we were awakened by loud scrapes and crashes. There were bears digging through the garbage outside our window! My grandmother reassured us that we would be okay; the bears were just looking for some food, and would soon be on their way. She made us feel so safe.

Years later, when I was in my early thirties, I attended a five-day transformational workshop with one of my mentors. The moment I met my roommate, I knew there was divine orchestration at play: she was a mirror image of my grandmother, and had the same loving, nurturing demeanor.

On the second day of the workshop, I was being held by one of the assistants as my mentor worked with another participant in the center of the circle. Suddenly, I was jolted into the most vivid memory of my life.

> *I am at Kaaps Chocolate Shoppe with Grandma and Mom. We are sitting in the big booths with the deep mahogany wood. It is early evening, and we are eating hot fudge sundaes in the tall glass dishes that are so sparkly and beautiful. Our spoons clank on the glass as we eat. Others in the shop are talking; I hear the murmur of their voices. I am happy to be here, sharing ice cream with the two women I love so much.*

This memory opened the floodgates for a powerful surge of both grief and gratitude that I didn't know was stored so deeply in my body. It was an opening for deep healing, and I spent the remaining two-and-a-half days of the retreat processing it. I let the grief that I'd had to submerge as a child come fully to the surface to be felt, and released.

This healing was a divine gift from my Grandma.

After that experience, I began to connect powerfully with Grandma's spirit, particularly during Breathwork (a powerful healing modality that uses conscious breathing patterns to release old emotions and open people to deeper spiritual connection).

I remember one session, during which I was feeling grief over my grandma not having a happy life. She was in an abusive relationship with my grandpa, and had used alcohol to cope with what was happening. She eventually left the marriage after twenty-five years, but ended up getting breast cancer and dying in her early fifties. As I wept, I heard her say to me, *"Shelley, my life wasn't all bad. I had some really happy times too; I want you to know that. I loved to travel with your grandpa. One of my favorite places was Hawaii. You should take a trip there; I think you would love it, too!"*

At times, I feel my grandmother's spirit near me, and say to myself, "Oh! Grandma's here." The first time that happened, I was lying in bed. I felt her presence so strongly that I started to talk with her in my mind. It was so comforting to connect with her again, and brought to mind the times she'd held me while I slept.

In the morning, I said to myself, "If that really happened—if I really connected with Grandma again—please give me a sign!"

Later that day, I went through the bank drive-thru, and connected with my favorite teller, Deb. Along with my receipt, Deb sent back a small Milky Way candy bar in the container.

"I *love* Milky Way bars!" I exclaimed. "My grandma used to give these to me when I was a little girl!"

And then, I smiled to myself, because I'd just received the confirmation I had asked for. I really had connected with my grandma the night before.

Thank you, Grandma, for being my first spiritual mentor, and for continuing to love me, support me, and walk with me as I explore my journey here on Earth. I know we will be together again when at last I make my transition to the spiritual realm.

Who was your first spiritual mentor?

_____

_____

_____

_____

Do you ever feel your departed loved ones close to you during your day?
What are the messages they share with you?

_____

_____

_____

_____

What was the last spiritual "sign" that you received? What action did it
validate, or prompt you to take?

_____

_____

_____

_____

The Lake House

Suzanne Moore

*I*f I close my eyes, I can still smell the bilge of my father's wooden boat, and hear the gurgling sound of its engine puttering across the water. I can imagine myself at any age in its presence. My memories from the summers we spent at Silver Lake in New Hampshire are among my earliest.

When I was seven, my parents were fortunate enough to be able to buy a home there, right on the west shoreline, in a spot that was calm and sandy. My father would say it was the "preferred" side of the lake because we didn't have the sunset in our eyes in the afternoon.

Each June, we left New Jersey the day after school ended. I remember the frenzy of packing up the cars for the seven-hour drive that would take us from our school-year routine to the routine of summer—from homework and after-school activities to carefree afternoons of swimming and boating.

My father was a very generous man, and he shared his favorite place in the world with anyone and everyone he could. This sometimes meant having one set of guests leave in the morning, and new ones arrive in the afternoon. (As you might imagine, Mom only put up with that for a few summers.)

When I got a little older, I resented having to spend so much time at the lake. I wanted to be with my school friends, and go to the summer vacation spots they did. But then, as I was entering my teenage years—at about the time when many girls feel as though they have no friends—I made some of the best friends of my life.

We summer friends found each other at the lake, and we spent those teenage years together. Waterskiing and tubing filled our sunny

137

days, and playing ping-pong, Canasta, and pool filled the rainy ones.
Mine was the home where we spent the most time. It was the largest,
and could accommodate our crew. My parents were always happy to
have the gang floating in and out. Friends were greeted with a smile
and an offering, and reminded to return soon whenever they left.

There were legendary annual events, full of laughter and stories
told and retold. They were the kinds of experiences that form bonds
between generations, where friends become family, and family
members become best friends. My father would often stand back and
smile at these gatherings, happy to be the catalyst for such special
moments and to share the space that meant so much to him. He loved
to bring people together.

He also loved to provide. Often, he assured my brother and me
that he'd taken pains so we'd never have to sell our lakeside home.
But you know what they say: "You make plans, God laughs."

A summer came when my father struggled to cover his beloved
wood boat. He no longer had control of his balance. Gradually, many
of the tasks he'd taken deep pride in for years began to slip. We learned
he had Alzheimer's, and that his time on the lake was coming to an end.

We watched his ability to enjoy the lake and our home dwindle.
And as we did, it also became apparent that we would not own our
Silver Lake home for another generation.

I maximized the time I had left there. My children, my dog, and
I spent weeks at the lake, even when it was challenging to do so. My
husband drove hours back and forth each summer weekend so that we
could grasp the moments still available to us.

We visited the friends I'd played with as a teenager, renewing
those relationships and watching a new generation form similar bonds.
I tried to love every minute, but there was a shadow over all of it: the
knowledge that this place, one of the cornerstones of my life, would
no longer be a part of it.

Those last few summers, there were always tears behind my eyes.
I reminded myself that losing the house didn't mean losing the lake
and the relationships. I tried to convince myself that this could still be
the place that filled my cup every summer.

For much of my life, I'd made fun of my father for his love of the lake, his steadfast desire to be nowhere else. Yet, as I sat in that house, holding his hand while he took his last breath, I realized that I felt exactly the same. The lake had become to me what it had been to him: the touchstone around which all other parts of my life occur.

A few months ago, I drove to the lake house for one last weekend; one last hurrah with the cousins who have spent countless hours there with us. As anticipated, a lot of the drive included tears—but the tears felt different this time. Instead of sadness and longing, I felt a tremendous sense of peace and gratitude.

My mind replayed the years, the relationships, the stories. I thought about the friendships—not just my own—that grew during the time spent in our home. I remembered leaning across the island in the kitchen to snatch a bite of food, and gazing out over the lake on quiet evenings from the shelter of the screened-in porch.

Instead of sadness, I cried at my good fortune. I found myself in awe that, out of all the people in this world, I was among those to have owned that home, to have been a catalyst for so many friendships and wonderful memories. I have never felt so humbled, and so favored.

I've read about gratitude and what it can do for the heart and soul, but until that evening, driving to the lake house for the last time, I didn't really understand it. I felt a peace and a confidence I've never felt before: a knowing that all would be okay.

And so it is.

Since that last trip, I feel as though I have had a rebirth. I've released old wounds, some of which have nothing to do with the house. I am living each day with a sense of clarity I've never known before.

It feels strange to write it, but it's as though by experiencing a new level of gratitude I stripped away a cloak I'd been living in. I see everything with new eyes, and can instantly tap into the state of grace I felt in the car that night. I am released from the sadness not just of the house sale, but of losing my dad in such a belabored way.

The house is now sold, and as I write this, I'm looking ahead to the first summer I can remember without it. Mom's move kept her close to the lake and we will spend a portion of this summer with her. No doubt there will be hours of boating and swimming. The dear friendships will continue, as will the laughter and stories and visits with our cousins.

But the sounds on the water at night, the peaceful energy of the porch, and the shoreline that holds so many memories ... They now belong to a new family.

It's true that we never know what we have until it's gone—but it's also true that the release of one thing makes us ready to receive something new.

I am so grateful for the life that was my father's, and for the love he had for Silver Lake. It's a love that became mine too—and in so doing, it has charted the path of my life. And while it is now forever altered, I am at peace with the transition, and feel ready to accept the new experiences that can come to me as a result.

Reflection

What are the constants in your life? How would a shift in them affect you?

_____

_____

_____

_____

When has your anticipation of a sad event clouded your ability to enjoy the present? What can you be aware of next time this happens?

_____

_____

_____

_____

What in your life has seemed like a burden, only to become something beautiful and treasured?

_____

141

_____

_____

_____

CHAPTER
Five

Grace is ...
Breathing Through It

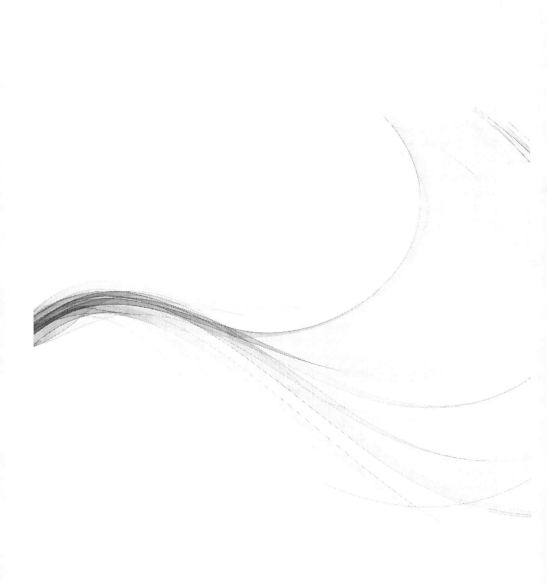

Hands Off the Wheel

Kellyann Schaefer

I watched in horror as the team of doctors stood over my son's listless little body. I screamed aloud—I wanted to kill someone. Well, not really kill someone, but *do something*, make something happen. I was so distraught, I could barely hold on any longer.

We'd been sitting vigil at my son's side for six days now. Just ten minutes before, my son had looked over at us and smiled—but then, his gaze started to drift off, as if he was disconnecting from reality. He stopped responding to us; he just stared at the ceiling above him. I ran out the door, screaming for help. My husband stood there, trying to remain stoic as he tried again and again to get our son to respond. There was nothing. No response.

***

Had it really been only ten days since this drama began? It felt like a lifetime.

Our son had been sick for four very long days before we brought him to the hospital. Twice in those four days, we'd been assured by our local emergency room doctors that it was "just viral," but I knew this was more than just the average flu.

Within four hours of arriving at the Children's Hospital, my son—my joyful, smart, loving son, whose mission in life is to "hug people" and "help the world see that love cures all"—was about to go into surgery.

I had known. Somehow, I'd known. But still, a part of me died when they told us what they'd found on the CT scan: a large cranial abscess that required emergency surgery. He would have three teams of specialists in the operating room with him. Three teams to meticulously clear out the abscess from his brain, his sinuses, and behind his right eye.

Hour after hour, for the next six hours, they updated us as they worked diligently to save his life.

After surgery, he seemed to be recovering well. His little body valiantly fought the infection wreaking havoc within him. With his head still wrapped in bandages, the drain to remove excess blood and fluid still in place, four separate IVs in his thin arms, and his head wrapped tightly to help reduce the swelling and stop the bleeding, he tried to reassure us that he was okay. He tried to share his love with us, as he always did, even though his face was so brutally swollen he couldn't even open his eyes.

As the days passed, he seemed to get stronger. But we were watching the numbers, and he was still very sick. The infection was still there, despite the four different IV antibiotics pumping through his body. The fevers continued, despite all the prayers we said over and over, and all the prayers of thousands of friends and strangers around the world.

He started losing the ability to use his left side. The paralysis started out in his toes, and then spread to his foot, his ankle, and his shin. As each hour passed, his mobility got worse. His left side no longer worked. He couldn't stand on his own. He could only hug me with one arm.

And on the sixth day after his surgery, when he drifted away to stare unresponsively at the ceiling, when his eyes rolled back in his head and the doctors and nurses surrounded him, when I saw my exhausted husband trying to be strong at his side, I couldn't bear it any longer. I no longer wanted to be part of this world, if my son did not survive.

And there was absolutely nothing I could do.

I collapsed on the floor in the hallway with tears streaming down my face. "I just want to die," I told the social worker who'd come to comfort me.

My husband came out a few minutes later.

"He's okay," he said, with a sigh of relief. "He had a seizure, but now he's okay. He's asleep."

I took a breath. We were past this hurdle—but what else was still to come? I was simultaneously grateful for the medical background my husband and I share, and afraid of what I knew. With comprehension of the processes also came the understanding of the long-term problems that could result from what was happening, and all of the other things that could go wrong from this point.

As my husband helped me off the floor, and told me that they were taking our son for another CT Scan—his fourth in six days—and that he would likely need to go back into surgery.

I almost collapsed again. How could my little guy possibly endure having his body opened up again? He was so tiny, so frail. He'd already lost ten pounds—twenty percent of his total body weight! How would he have the strength?

My husband went along for the scan, and I began to pace the hallways—a routine I was all too familiar with at this point. Back and forth, back and forth, as I prayed harder and harder, and got more and more angry. How could this have happened? Hadn't we been through enough already?

Angrier and angrier. More and more frightened.

The voices of fear crept in. *"He's going to die,"* they whispered. *"He'll never be the same again."* The darkness swept over and through me. I felt like I was battling Hell itself.

I couldn't stand the hallways any longer, so I went to the cafeteria for a cup of tea. "How dare you get tea?" the voices raged. I tried to squeeze them out of my head with hands clasped on either side of my skull. I fought the entire way to the cafeteria, with everything I had. I was fighting for my son's life inside my own head. I was fighting for my family. I was fighting for "normalcy."

But it wasn't enough.

The walk down the hallway from the elevators to the cafeteria was the longest of my life. It was as if I was walking to my own execution: my head down, my chest tight, numbness overtaking me. Inside me was only this battle of light and dark, of faith and fear. I'd been fighting those voices for days, trying to be more powerful than they were, trying to tap into all that I was, and all that I knew—but now, they were all I could hear. *"He's surely going to die. He won't be coming home with you."* I had been fighting those voices for days. Trying to be more powerful than they were. Trying to tap into all that I was. But I was so tired. I was tired of the fighting, and tired of trying to control the outcome. I could no longer carry this weight on my shoulders. Physically, mentally, and emotionally, I no longer had the strength.

And then, suddenly, I knew.

Alone, I would lose this fight. I *had* to let go. I had to believe that something stronger and more powerful would step in to assist me, my son, and my family.

And so, I did the only thing left for me to do: *I let go.*

I closed my eyes tightly, and imagined I was handing over my steering wheel to God. I totally let go of control. There was nothing else in this physical world that I could do to help my son.

"It's your job now," I told God. "It's your job to make sure he comes home safe to me."

The voices stopped dead, as if by magic. In their place was quiet—a profound stillness like I have never felt before. I took a deep breath, filling my lungs with the hospital air, and knew, for the first time since our nightmare began, that everything was going to be okay.

I did not go into grace easily. I fought it as hard as I could, until I had nothing left to fight with. And yet, when I handed over that imaginary wheel—and my son's life—to a higher power, I had no doubt that grace had stepped in.

***

Now, I look back on those weeks as if they aren't real. After twenty days in the hospital, my son came home with us. Aside from the healing scar across his head, you would never know the turmoil he suffered, or imagine that we almost lost him—not once but twice in six days.

The seizure that finally pushed me to the edge of grace was, in fact, an enormous blessing, because it forced the doctors to take him back to surgery. Despite what any of us wanted, it was what his body needed. This extra attention, so frightening in the moment, was what enabled him to fully recover.

I still haven't had the chance to deeply understand the how or why of what happened to my son. Despite the fact that my prayers were answered, it may take years for me to feel that he is safe. What will I do the first time he has a headache? The first time he has a fever, or falls down? I'm not sure. But I will remember that God and His angels are watching out for us, because that divine light shines out of my son's eyes every time he wraps his little arms around me and says, "I love you, Mom. I'm okay now."

In moments of crisis, do you feel like you have to control or manage everything?

_____

_____

_____

_____

When was the last time you truly surrendered to grace? What did it take to bring you to that point?

_____

_____

_____

_____

What would happen if you "handed over the wheel" in your daily life? What would it feel like to be led instead of leading?

_____

_____

_____

_____

House of Grace

Beth Marshall

*Y*ou are Live ;) Welcome to this phase of The Revelation Project.

I swallowed hard and took a deep breath. Now that I'd seen the e-mail's subject line, there was no turning back. It was time to look myself in the eye, and allow others to fully see me.

I went in search of the pictures from my photo shoot from the month before. I've never been one who loves the camera, and I'd only recently learned to appreciate my beauty. Now, I had trusted three women I'd just met to select pictures they thought best "revealed" me, and I had agreed to share those pictures with the world *before I had even seen them.*

With one eye open and the other in a cautious half-squint, I scanned the photos. During the shoot itself, I had felt courageous, playful, beautiful, vulnerable, and powerful, and I hoped some of those feelings would show.

Slowly but surely, a smile turned up on my lips.

The day before I saw the photos was one of the worst I could remember, with sadness and anger flowing in at full force. I railed against the Universe, yelling, "What more do you want from me? I am *so done* with things feeling difficult!" (Yeah, it was one of *those* days. I swore and yelled so much in the span of an hour that I had to take a five-hour nap out of sheer exhaustion.)

In stark contrast to my temper tantrum of the day before, I was now literally face-to-face with undeniable evidence of my divinity and grace. The Universe had heard my expletive-laden rant, and had answered with a photographic reflection of myself I could no longer deny.

Gorgeous. Bold. Beautiful. Uninhibited. Stunning. Sensual. Sexy. Radiant. Joyful. Courageous. Vibrant. Empowered. Powerful. Playful. Authentic. Vulnerable. Fun. Divine.

These were words people used to describe me in the photos. I intentionally allowed in each word. Many of these were things I'd never considered to be part of who I was—and I most certainly hadn't experienced myself this way during my emotional fit the day before.

In the months leading up to the photo shoot, I'd been on top of the world. After a challenging year of ups and downs, it finally seemed as if I was hitting my stride. I was in the flow of manifesting my dreams: things were shifting, opportunities were arriving, and I felt powerfully open to the future even though my path was taking some unexpected twists and turns.

I was also looking forward to my first real vacation in six years. It was going to be the trip of a lifetime. Only days after the shoot, I was heading to Bali with a group of incredibly powerful women and friends. I felt like I deserved some rejuvenation after so many fast-paced years of personal growth.

The shoot itself was fun and relaxed. I felt light in my body; my heart opened wide and allowed me to play and explore.

Once we touched down in paradise, though, the proverbial shit began to hit the fan.

I was miserably hot, which regularly threw me off-center. I felt disoriented, and consistently mindful of what I needed at any given time—whether that was water, food, rest, or something else. There were moments where my body and mind did not seem to be my own. I manifested the most powerfully active menstrual cycle I've had in thirty years, and there were mornings when I awoke in tears with absolutely no explanation.

There was a definite purification happening, physically and emotionally. I knew it, and so I did my best to appreciate the moments of joy, beauty, connection, and peace through the barrage of distraction. But I'd be lying if I said my gratitude practice was working, because it wasn't.

I was supposed to be in paradise, spending time with amazing women and witnessing the spiritual magic of Bali that I'd heard so much about. So ... What the hell?

The cycle was endlessly frustrating. I'd breathe myself into center by focusing on gratitude, and think, *Okay, I'm good.* Then—*Wait, what just happened? Why am I angry?* Breathe some more. Focus on the beauty and peace around me. *Dammit, now I'm sad.* My emotions were all over the map, and I couldn't find my center for longer than a New York minute.

"Why can't I keep my inner peace?" I asked myself. "Where's the grace in all of this?"

Grace has been in my life since my birth. Even my name, Beth Ann, translates as "house of grace." All of this drama just wasn't my style. I felt like a tsunami was rising inside me, and I was trying to contain it.

The big wave finally unleashed itself one night as I walked back from dinner. We'd dined beachside in the moonlight, which was lovely, but to return to our villa we had to hike back up the scariest stairs I've ever encountered. After several flights, I crashed into a heap on the stairs in complete emotional breakdown. Gushing tears by the bucket, unable to breathe, I wanted desperately to be in the comfort of my home instead of terrified and disoriented across the world.

The rest of the trip was a blur. I summoned the courage to continue climbing so I could get back to our villa, but I was done fighting. I was emotional toast.

Five days later, I began my journey home. Upon arriving, I was gentle with myself as I worked through jet lag and the lingering impact of my intense emotions. I was as honest with myself as I could be about the lessons to be learned from this breakdown, and allowed more feelings to emerge without understanding much of what was happening—until I saw my pictures a week later, and the pieces began to fall into place.

The woman staring back at me from the photos was freedom and power personified. I had allowed all of me to shine that day, and the photographer had captured my soul.

It delighted me. It also scared the living shit out of me.

Now everyone would see *her*. They would know that, even with past successes, I was playing small compared to what was possible. They would know this because *I* knew it.

The realization hit me like a ton of bricks. I had left my photo shoot on an absolute high, but I had no idea how to *be* the woman I'd been at the photo shoot in real life. Instead, I'd unconsciously detached myself from the powerful experience I'd had, and safely tucked her away in my heart as I had many times before.

Except, this time, the Universe had other plans. Waiting for me in Bali were nine other powerful women who showed up like a walking wall of mirrors. Individually and collectively, these women reflected back every part of who I was and who I could become. It was challenging for me to see another woman be bold while I held myself back. It was upsetting to see another woman powerfully own her talents when I hadn't yet owned mine. It was unnerving to see a woman's vibrant, joyful, and playful nature when I hadn't allowed myself that same freedom.

Apparently it wasn't just the Balinese heat and humidity that had been suffocating my body. My resistance to fully owning my own greatness had been suffocating my Soul, and she was screaming from the inside.

Unintentionally, I had tried to contain the woman who had finally come out to play at the photo shoot. No wonder I was exhausted, disoriented, and agitated! Even my Boston accent, which was more noticeable than usual in the casual setting of the trip, left me feeling somewhat vulnerable as it was noticed by the other women.

I cried in relief as I realized I wasn't crazy (because I'd honestly thought I was losing it). I had simply been resistant, and I could remedy that by seeing the gift I hadn't yet been willing to receive. It isn't about figuring out who I *should* be: I am simply supposed to *be*. It is time for my Soul to live freely, abundantly, and joyfully. It is time to allow my grace to breathe and flourish in the world. It is time to unabashedly unleash all of my power.

While I'm still finding my way in my new world of freedom, I know now that I have the ability to find my grace over and over again, even when chaos surrounds me. By focusing on gratitude for everything (including the hard moments), I've found the gateway to the lessons of life, and ultimately, my own personal house of grace.

And, because of the revelations of a photo shoot coupled with a trip to the other side of the world, I am choosing to confidently and gracefully own my gifts and step up to change the world as I only I can.

Have you ever truly seen the woman you are? What was the experience like for you?

_____

_____

_____

_____

When you are around other powerful women, how do you feel? What can your reaction tell you about your relationship to yourself and your own power?

_____

_____

_____

_____

What can you learn from your challenging emotions? What do they have to tell you about your own evolution?

_____

_____

_____

_____

With Open Eyes

Dr. Colleen Georges

I couldn't breathe. I felt like I had a heavy weight pressing against my lungs and my heart was racing. I thought I might be developing asthma in my twenties. However, after talking with a few friends who had asthma, it was clear that I was experiencing something very different.

Perhaps it would've been obvious to someone else, but to me, a woman working on my doctorate in counseling psychology, I somehow couldn't see that I was experiencing panic attacks.

I'd lived with anxiety for many years before it escalated to that level. Ruminating over past decisions I'd made, replaying scenarios, and imagining what I could've done or said to change outcomes had long been a habit of mine. I'd mentally run through the details of things I wished I hadn't done over and over, as if thinking about them could change the past. I beat myself up over ways I believed I'd failed in relationships, school, and work, and I felt sorry for myself because of all of the things that (I perceived) had gone wrong for me.

Since I felt like I'd done so much wrong in the past, I often had a bleak outlook on the future. I worried about what could go wrong in my romantic relationships. I worried about not doing well on papers and exams in school. I worried that I wouldn't be successful in my career. I worried about being late when I had somewhere to go. I worried that people wouldn't like me. I worried about *everything*. And because I worried, I played out all possible scenarios of what was to come in the hope that I could somehow control it.

I spent so much time in the past and future, regretting and catastrophizing, that I missed most of the here and now.

In addition to worry and anxiety, there were other ways I lived my life with a deficit mentality. It's a great irony that my gift as a person and counselor is my innate ability to see the good in others, and inspire them to see it too—and yet, I couldn't seem to see the good in myself. I never believed that I was good enough.

Not only did I believe I wasn't good enough, I also thought I didn't *have* enough. I thought about how I didn't have the job, money, house, and other things I *needed* to be happy, and felt envious of what others had that I didn't.

It was these negative thinking habits that ultimately led me to that panicked moment when I couldn't breathe—a moment which would be the first of many. I suffered with progressively more frequent panic attacks for nearly two years.

Ultimately, I found myself searching for answers in the place that made the most sense to me: the bookstore. I honestly had no idea what I was looking for, but believed I'd know it when I saw it. Then, a title jumped right out at me—*Gratitude: A Way of Life*, by Louise Hay. I hadn't previously thought much about gratitude. I'm not sure why it struck me so much, but I bought the book. I went home and began reading the stories that filled the pages—stories about people who had transformed their lives simply by being thankful. Could that really be possible? I thought it was worth a try.

I started trying to count my blessings before bed at night. It wasn't easy at all at first. No monumentally amazing things had happened to me. Did that mean that there was nothing to be grateful for? I didn't want to give up, though, so I decided that if big great things hadn't happened, maybe small great things had.

I started paying attention during the day—and suddenly, I saw it. Someone opened a door for me at the store. Another person let me make a left turn while driving. I had a nice conversation with a stranger in line while getting coffee. *Huh.* Those little things made me feel great in the moment, especially when I let myself ponder that they didn't *have* to happen. They happened because someone *chose* to be kind and friendly, and that was actually pretty amazing.

Weeks went by, and I kept seeing more good. I noticed how the birds sounded in the morning, how beautiful the trees really were, and how magnificent the summer air could feel when I first stepped outside. The experience of awe became a regular occurrence.

I realized how blessed I was to have wonderful family and friends, to be getting an advanced education, to have several jobs that were helping to finance that education, and to be doing work I loved and which helped others. It helped me to see that *I* was good, *I* had purpose, *I* was enough. Gratitude showed me that some of my greatest gifts from God have been provided through my challenges, which gave me wisdom I could use and share.

I finally realized that, with faith in God's plan (even when we don't immediately understand it), we no longer have need for worry.

God's grace, people's graciousness, and gifts to be grateful for had always been there, right in front of me, but I'd been so focused on what I perceived to be mistakes, problems, and potential catastrophes that I hadn't opened up my eyes wide enough to see all the good within and around me.

Over a few months of daily gratitude practice, my long-standing negative thinking progressively washed away; it was like some crazy kind of magic. Envy, self-hatred, pessimism, rumination, catastrophizing, worry, and anxiety disintegrated. My panic attacks completely disappeared, and have never returned. Calm, confident, content, and self-compassionate became my normal.

I've been living my life by the virtue of gratitude and grace for fifteen years now. Saying "thank you" to God, and to all who provide me a service or kindness, is automatic. Gratitude is no longer a practice I must remind myself to engage in, but simply a way of life. It no longer takes effort to see all the good, it takes effort *not* to, because I know in my heart that God's grace will prevail.

The practice of gratitude also helped to shape my career trajectory. Once I became focused on all of the good within and around us, practicing traditional therapy and diagnosing people's limitations wasn't aligned with my values. I wanted to diagnose people's strengths and resources. I wanted to help others see *their* good. I immediately integrated this practice into my work with my therapy clients and college student advisees, and ultimately launched my own practice in Positive Psychology, a field which utilizes the practices of gratitude, kindness, forgiveness, self-compassion, optimism, and strengths identification to help people flourish.

Today, as a Positive Psychology coach, community wellness group leader, and university faculty member, I witness gratitude changing the lives of my clients and students, just as it did mine. Counting daily blessings is a staple of the work we do together, and it keeps working its infinite magic.

Gratitude's impact on my life, as well as my clients' and students' lives, is more than enough evidence of its power—but I see the most beautiful magic with my son. Josh is six-and-a-half years old, and when he was just under five-and-a-half, I began practicing gratitude with him. Acknowledging what we are grateful for each day is a central part of our bedtime ritual.

I started by asking him to think of three things he was thankful for that day. Much like me, Josh had a hard time coming up with more than one thing when we first began our gratitude ritual. When he did list things, they were often material items: "I'm thankful you bought me a toy today. I'm thankful I have lots of toys. I'm thankful I got a cool goodie bag at the party." Today, however, he rattles off ten or more things he's grateful for, often saying things like, "I'm thankful that I got to go to school today. I'm thankful I have a great mom and dad. I'm thankful I played with my cousins today. I'm thankful God made us a beautiful world." Profound for a first grader!

Last year, Josh told me that he wanted to keep God's world beautiful—so could we clean it up? So we did, and he's since requested that we do our community clean-up annually. We also show our gratitude for simple blessings by volunteering twice a month at our local food pantry.

All of us have something to give and be grateful for. Today, reader, I'm grateful to share this story in a beautiful book that could transform your life—just as my life was transformed by such a book fifteen years ago.

When we look narrowly for the negative, the negative is what we'll find. Yet, when we open our eyes wide enough to see all the good, our blessings will unceasingly abound.

Reflection

Do you have a gratitude practice? Can you think of three things to be grateful for today?

_____

_____

_____

_____

Who are you most grateful for in your life, and why?

_____

_____

_____

_____

What challenges have you endured that you can be grateful for today because they've given you wisdom?

162

_____

_____

_____

_____

Our Hidden Angels

Alex Bratty

I was slumped on the floor, arms around my knees, weeping uncontrollably. It was supposed to be a quick shower and cry. But once the faucet sprayed open, so did I. Out came breath-stealing sobs: I couldn't stop.

Just a few months prior, we had heard those three dreaded words, "You have cancer."

We had actually been grateful for the diagnosis. It had taken months of testing while my husband was getting sicker and weaker. At least now we knew what we were dealing with. As we sat in the oncologist's office learning about the intensive treatment ahead, my priorities snapped into place. I'd just made partner in my firm, but work would have to take a back seat. My only focus would be getting him better.

Even before treatment began we faced adversity. During a test to make sure his lung capacity could handle the upcoming chemotherapy, he collapsed. He was rushed to the closest emergency room followed by ten days in the hospital being treated for pneumonia.

It didn't get easier. Just after the first grueling chemo session, he experienced what physicians call "dangerous" side effects. The doctor was firm on the phone, "If you don't get him to an ER right now he could die!" When I gasped, "But how can I do that? There's a blizzard outside and already three feet of snow!" He shot back, "That's what 9-1-1 is for. Do it *now!*"

We were rescued from our home by ambulance, and my husband was placed in isolation at the hospital, lest any germs infiltrate his floundering immune system. His stay was broken after two weeks only by the need to return for the second round of chemo.

163

After that, the side effects were awful, but not life-threatening. Progress.

Yet, none of this was why I was bawling in the fetal position. I'd managed to hold it together those past few months because my husband was hopeful and fighting with all he had. We were a team, and we could make it.

Over the last week, though, the energy had shifted. He'd had mid-treatment tests to make sure the chemo was working, the results of which were sent to his internist of thirty years, and to the oncologist. The first call came from the family doctor, "Great news! The report says no visible cancer cells. You are on the road to recovery!"

Wow. We were both elated … and confused. We were only halfway through a six-month treatment plan. How could he be cured so quickly?

As we drove to the oncologist's office three days later my husband was more hopeful than ever. "Maybe we're done. Maybe he'll say it's cleared up faster than expected, and there will be no more chemo. I'm actually looking forward to going there today!"

I nodded and "uh-huhed," but I had a pit in my stomach. Somehow I knew that wasn't the case. Unfortunately, I was right; during our appointment, the oncologist dryly stated, "The report shows solid progress, so we'll continue as planned."

My husband was stunned. "What? What do you mean? My other doctor said the cancer was gone. Surely I'm done. How can I need three more months of this?"

The response was stern, "He's right – we can no longer see cancer cells. That just means they've shrunk to a microscopic size. If we stop now, they *will* come back. Treatment has to continue—and yes, you need the full course."

We shuffled down the hallway to endure the longest, saddest day of chemo yet.

The drive home was silent at first. Then, it began. "Why do I have to keep doing this? It's killing me. I can barely make it from the bed to the armchair to the bathroom. Three more months of this? I just can't take it!"

What could I say? The illness and treatment had stolen my vibrant, Type-A, ready-for-anything husband and left behind a weak shell of his former self. I tried to find the right words, but they all fell short.

As the next few days passed, he became more despondent; his strong mental attitude was replaced with negativity and anger. I tried multiple things to lift his spirit: I wrote him funny poems, and created a photo collage of happier times for him to look at from bed. He appreciated the effort, but the dark cloud remained.

By Sunday morning, I couldn't bear it anymore. I had to crack, but I couldn't let him see it. So there I was, stranded in the shower, desperately praying to God for answers. When I finally got out and looked at my swollen face in the mirror, the reply came: *It's time to drop the Superwoman façade. You can't do it all yourself. You need help, advice, and support.*

I dressed and fired off e-mails; the first went to the wife of one of my business partners. She had nursed her husband back to life from a quadruple-bypass surgery—surely she had some wisdom to impart. One went to his family, urging them to send cards since opening mail had become a highlight for him in his incapacitated state. Another went to his buddies, asking them to check in, and please to coordinate so the calls didn't all come at once.

The replies came flooding in. "Alex, of course! What else do you need? You know we are here for you—please just ask."

I realized in that moment how much I had cut us off from our world. At the beginning, our friends and family had called all the time. They wanted to visit, but I declined because his red blood cell count was so low that exposure to even the common cold could be life-threatening. I'd thanked everyone for their kind offers of help, but politely refused each of them, saying that I was good, and that we would be fine. And we had been, until now.

That week I was blessed by the touches of multiple angels. The calls came in, the cards arrived. His mood buoyed a little. But the real breakthrough came from the e-mail my partner's wife sent. "Give him a project. He needs something he can own again so he feels useful." It was a gift from heaven—and in that instant, I understood.

Before he got sick, my husband had enjoyed a long and successful career as a serial entrepreneur, beloved by clients and staff and revered by his peers. Now, he couldn't even leave the house unless it was for a medical appointment—and even then, he needed my assistance. Was it any wonder he was mired in gloom?

I knew exactly what the project would be. I have never been a fan of gardening, but he was, and spring was coming. The yard was a mess, and he would normally be getting ready to weed, mulch, and plant beautiful flowers. He obviously couldn't do that now, but he could be the supervisor. I had him make the list of tasks. He would call to order the mulch, and we'd pay to have someone do the weeding. I could handle the flowers.

He sat on the stoop directing me, "Dig deeper before you plant. That one doesn't look right. We need better colors over here. Which ones are you going to put in this area?" Part of me wanted to retort, "Can you just let me work in peace and check in later?" But a greater part of me was smiling. This one little project had brought meaning and fulfillment. Mentally and emotionally, my husband was back!

As we moved through those final months of treatment, the physical toll worsened, yet we were stronger than ever. We were fighting together again, and we had a team of angels bolstering us. Homemade meals were delivered to our doorstep unsolicited, friends stopped by my office to say hi and drop off goodies, and the cards and calls never ended.

We now live every day in gratitude for his good health and for every person who touched us along the way—from the parking attendant at the oncologist's office who knew when to bring the car around so we didn't have to wait, to the amazing medical personnel who always reserved a private chemo room without asking because they knew I wasn't going anywhere during those day-long treatments, to our family and friends who lifted us in ways they simply can't imagine.

There, by the grace of God and our angels, did we survive and thrive.

Reflection

Do you feel comfortable asking for help? Why or why not?

_____

_____

_____

_____

How can you feel and express even greater gratitude for those in your family and community who help you and your loved ones every day?

_____

_____

_____

_____

Healing isn't always just a process within the body. What can you do to give someone close to you a greater sense of purpose, and facilitate their healing?

_____

_____

_____

_____

All Is Well

Kelley Grimes, MSW

"What do you dream of doing?"
This question was asked by my mentor at her Mindset Retreat. Curious to see what would emerge, I picked up my pen. But the words which appeared on the page in front of me weren't the ones I was expecting.

I want to travel to Australia to visit my daughter.

Until that moment, I had not been conscious of my deep desire to go see my daughter. The awareness brought tears to my eyes; this dream came directly from my heart rather than my head.

Eight months earlier, my beloved eighteen-year-old daughter Fiona had followed her lifelong dream of traveling to Australia. After suffering chronic health challenges for most of her life—and still suffering from a chronic daily migraine that had lasted four years—she decided to take a gap year and travel after graduating from high school.

I was deeply inspired by her courageous choice to follow her dream, as well as by the belief in herself that enabled her to venture so far from California on her own.

As soon as Fiona made the decision to travel, I knew that I needed to embrace the difficult spiritual practice of letting go. Much of my identity was deeply rooted in the myriad roles I played in her life: I was parent, medical coordinator, health and school advocate, counselor, and teacher. We had been through so much together: having her move halfway across the world would undoubtedly transform my life.

Fortunately, I was able to find meaning in Fiona's desire to go to Australia. I saw this trip as her opportunity to heal herself. When, after traveling for a few months, she'd asked me to come visit, I decided it

169

would be better to use the money to help her to stay longer, since she was so happy living there.

In truth, I had buried my own dream of traveling the world deep within my heart when I became pregnant with Fiona in graduate school. My husband and I had planned to travel to Europe when I received my Master of Social Work degree, but when I became unexpectedly pregnant, we put off our plans. After Fiona's first seizure at age two, I did not feel comfortable traveling far without her, and did not leave the country again.

Choosing to follow my dream and visit my daughter was both empowering and exhilarating. I planned an amazing two-week trip to all of Fiona's favorite places in Australia—including Sydney, the Gold Coast, and gorgeous Byron Bay. I even organized a trip to Steve Irwin's Zoo, which had inspired Fiona's dream when she was five years old. I reserved, and paid for, our flights and accommodations. We were both very excited to see each other; we saw this trip as closure to Fiona's healing journey. She had finally broken her migraine cycle and was feeling better more and more of the time.

Less than a month before I was to arrive, Fiona left on a trip to Bali with friends. She sent me a Facebook message before she left from the Melbourne airport, saying goodbye. I received it at a celebration for my younger daughter, so I messaged her wishes for a fabulous and safe trip and put my phone away.

When I arrived home a few hours later and opened my computer, I found dozens of messages from Fiona. The Australian Immigration official said she had overstayed her visa and would not be allowed back into the country for three years. She was scared and confused. Her last message simply said "HELP!"

I anxiously replied to her messages, but received no response. I was beside myself. Fear flooded through me and I felt totally helpless, not knowing if my daughter was being detained in Australia or was on a plane to Bali. Eight long hours passed before I found out that she had arrived safely in Bali.

For the next two weeks I advocated passionately for Fiona to be given a short stay visa to Australia. I followed every recommendation, sent substantiating documentation, and paid every fee. Meanwhile, Fiona was in a state of panic as her friends were returning home and she was alone in Bali. Worse, she was running low on money, and most of her belongings had been left in Australia.

We lived in an anxiety-inducing limbo, receiving no information from the Australian Immigration Department except an e-mail that they were reviewing her case. Each night we purchased a hotel room online for her, hoping she would be able to return to Australia the next day.

As the date of my flight to Sydney approached, my anxiety continued to grow. I was unable to focus on anything besides Fiona's predicament. My usual self-nurturing practices barely put a dent in my stress and overwhelm.

Then, two days before I was to leave for Australia, I awoke with the realization that I was giving away all of my power to the Australian Immigration Department. I had become so attached to my "dream vacation" that I had been unable to see the amazing adventure unfolding in front of me. I could continue wishing things would turn out as I had planned, or I could surrender to the flow.

In that moment, I was flooded with profound gratitude for my awareness of choice. I recognized that whether I ended up traveling through Australia or going to meet my daughter in Bali, having this opportunity to travel was truly a dream come true!

This shift in my thinking allowed me to view the entire experience as an adventure, and transformed my anxiety, fear, and disappointment into hope, joy, and gratitude. I was able to see all the blessings of this unexpected situation, and stop focusing on things I had no control over.

When I boarded my flight for Australia, I still did not know where I would end up, but I was at peace. I repeated my mantra, "All is well," over and over to myself. Focusing on everything I was grateful for allowed me to actually begin believing it.

My belief that all was well ignited my trust that my journey was unfolding exactly as it was meant to. As a result, I received the most spontaneous, unplanned international trip of my life.

The day after arriving in Sydney I had still heard nothing about

Fiona's visa—so, in less than an hour, I booked a flight to Bali and rented a villa a few blocks from the beach. The villa was called the Love Villa, and finding this treasure felt like another sign from the universe that I was heading to exactly where I was meant to be. I felt surrounded by grace, and buoyed by my gratitude.

Twenty-four hours later, Fiona and I were joyfully reunited in Bali at the Love Villa. The sweet smell of incense in the air, flowering plants all around, and the warm weather created an absolute paradise. I experienced a profound sense of returning home, and was overwhelmed with gratitude for the remarkable beauty and peacefulness of Bali.

The next morning, I awoke to find Fiona suffering from a terrible migraine. I attempted to support and comfort her, but after so many months apart, I did not want to fall back into my role of being solely responsible for resolving her pain and suffering. So, instead of hovering and growing anxious, I went for a walk on the beach.

As I walked, I reflected on the years Fiona had suffered with chronic pain. She'd taken great strides toward healing while in Australia; I wondered why this was happening now, while we were together in paradise.

As if the universe was answering my question, a Balinese man walked toward me wearing a shirt that read, in English, "All is well." Seeing my mantra on this man's shirt, I was moved to tears. I knew in that moment that *believing* "All is well" was the most healing thing I could do for Fiona. Embodying that wisdom allowed me to be grateful for being in paradise even as Fiona was suffering.

After a few days, Fiona's migraine receded. We spent the rest of our time in Bali exploring the island, practicing yoga in magical places, eating amazing food, and being in a state of awe and wonder for all the beauty around us.

In the end, the Australian Immigration Department confirmed that Fiona would not be allowed to re-enter Australia, even on a transit visa to gather her belongings and fly back home with me from Sydney, and so we rerouted her ticket to San Diego through Tokyo. As we parted at the airport in Bali, about to fly in totally different directions, we were deeply grateful. Our Balinese adventure had gifted us with the realization that we are always in paradise when we embrace the mindset that "All is well." To learn that empowering spiritual lesson in such a powerfully spiritual place amplified its meaning.

The gift of this incredible journey to Bali was the lesson that, no matter how life unfolds around me, all is well. Remembering this wisdom encourages me to stay in faith, be at peace, recognize the blessings, and connect with the joy available in each moment.

Reflection

How do worry and stress affect you in your daily life?

_____

_____

_____

_____

How would your life be different if you allowed yourself to believe that "All is well"?

_____

_____

_____

_____

What challenges or disappointments in your life have you been able to turn into opportunities?

_____

_____

_____

_____

Lifting the Fog

Bailey Frumen, MSW, LCSW

I was on the road to retirement. I had expected my career to last for twenty-five years, but after just seven, I was ready to move on.

When I started, the job sounded pretty good to me. As a driven, Type-A woman, I was used to working hard and deferring pleasure, play, and free time: after college, I had completed my two-year master's degree in just one year. The position as a school social worker seemed like a good gig—I would work from 8:00 a.m. to 3:00 p.m., have my summers off, and retire in just twenty-five years to do whatever I wanted. I signed on the dotted line.

But the job wasn't enough for me. While I enjoyed my time with my students, I wanted more. I felt called to help more people; I wanted to make a bigger impact.

I decided to pursue my Post-Master's licensure as a Psychotherapist. In just two years, I started my private practice while continuing to work full-time at the school. Within six months of opening my doors, I had a waiting list that lasted more than two years. I was *busy*. My days were filled with meetings and classroom observations at the school, and my nights and weekends with counseling others. Somewhere in the mix, I started to lose myself. Working sixty or seventy hours each week, I stopped going to yoga. Grabbing wine with girlfriends was a thing of the past, and my husband and I were on a first name basis with the Chinese delivery guy.

175

But I had made it, right? Wasn't this what I'd always wanted—to help others, to make a greater impact? From the outside, life looked pretty good: I had a beautiful new home, a handsome husband, two cute dogs, and a pretty fat bank account from all of the hours I had logged. Then, out of what seemed like the clear blue, I started having panic attacks.

They began at night. My eyes would blink open at 2:00 or 3:00 a.m., and I would find myself in a sweat, heart pounding in my chest, almost unable to breathe. My mind would race, filled with questions:

What am I doing?

Is this what I really want?

If it isn't what I want, then what do I really want?

I felt paralyzed in this sudden and unexpected place of fear. Why was this happening? Didn't I always do the right thing?

The panic attacks progressed, often striking while I was on my way from the school to my office. Pulling over the car, I would think, *I help people deal with this sort of thing, why is it happening to me?*

The truth was, I was taking care of everyone else but myself. Feeling stressed out, overwhelmed, and completely sleep-deprived, I finally relented and went to my doctor. After running some tests, she determined that I was suffering from adrenal fatigue—a very common complaint amongst those of us who overtax ourselves and don't make time for self-care.

Aside from some supplements and acupuncture, her recommendation was that I *slow down*. I nearly laughed. If I slowed down, who would do everything that I did? Who would help the kids at school? Who would help my clients? Who would keep the house running?

As I drove home from that appointment, I was struck by the realization that *I didn't know how to slow down*. I had been going at the pace of a racehorse for as long as I could remember, but I couldn't quite understand why. *Why* was I working at a breakneck and exhaustive pace? *Why* was I filling my days to the brim with no time for myself? Truth was, I had no idea.

I would love to tell you that this is the point when everything magically turned around—but it didn't. The panic attacks, the 3:00 a.m. what-am-I-doing-with-my-life sweats, and the seventy-hour work weeks continued because *I didn't change anything*. I took the supplements and went to acupuncture, but I did not change a single thing about the way I was living. I didn't have any answers to the questions that plagued me, so I just kept doing what I knew how to do: work.

Months later, I snuck into a yoga class when a client canceled her session. As I lay on my mat for meditation, the instructor recited a quote by Ralph Waldo Emerson: "A man is what he thinks about all day long."

Was this true? In that moment, I realized that all I thought about was how stressed and overwhelmed I felt. No wonder I was burnt out and exhausted! But if I didn't want to feel that way, I had to figure out how I *did* want to feel. I had to get clear about how I truly wanted my life to look. How did I want to spend my days, months, and years?

As if the panic attacks weren't enough, the question of what I wanted in life was nearly enough to put me into cardiac arrest.

That was the moment where gratitude and grace entered my life. Trying to rewrite my whole way of living and figure out what I wanted seemed as overwhelming a task as any I'd ever tackled. I knew that I needed to give myself permission to take time and figure it out; in other words, I needed to bestow upon myself the grace I would wish upon anyone else. Instead of judging myself for not having it all figured out, I needed to be thankful for the journey which had revealed this opportunity for change.

Instead of tackling the change head on, I broke it down into six manageable areas: physical health, mental/emotional health, spirituality, finances, relationships, and career.

As I found clarity in one area at a time, I realized one universal truth and common thread in my journey towards self-understanding: we grow in direct correlation to the depth of the questions we ask ourselves. Instead of continuing to run around putting out fires in my life, focusing on everyone else's needs first, I needed to take the time to ask myself the questions that would help me to grow into the person I was meant to become. 177

After six months of learning to slow down, look within, and start treating myself with the care I gave to everyone else, a new, unexpected reality revealed itself to me.

While I was born to help others, working at the school and having my private practice wasn't fulfilling my purpose or calling in the world. When I figured out my reason for being, it became very clear that my mission in the world was to help other ambitious women lift the fog when they are feeling stuck in their lives, and to find clarity and greater connection to their purposes so that they can take action and live lives they love. It also became evident that while I was very good at my job, I simply couldn't wait for retirement to start enjoying my life. Within days, I tendered my resignation to my bosses at the school.

The insight I achieved was so crystal-clear and invigorating that it felt like a bolt of lightning. I didn't want to live my life like a to-do checklist. I didn't want to wait to start asking myself the questions that would help me grow and connect to my purpose, and I certainly didn't want to wait any longer to start taking better care of myself. Above all else, I didn't want to wait one more minute to take action to fall absolutely, one hundred percent head-over-heels in love with my life.

That was three years ago—and now I motivate and inspire women through writing, coaching, and speaking to do the same thing I did. It wasn't quitting my job or burning my bra that helped me create my amazing life, but rather giving myself the grace to fall in love with the life that only *I* had the power to create.

Do you consider yourself a "busy" person? If so, why is being busy important to you?

_____

_____

_____

_____

What is your busyness covering up? Is there something that you're avoiding or putting off because you "don't have time"?

_____

_____

_____

_____

What do you think would happen if you allowed yourself to slow down and make room for the things you really want?

_____

_____

_____

_____

CHAPTER
Six

Grace is ...
Within Us

The Perfect Present

Karen Spaiches

I thought I had life tied up with a pretty little bow. I had a caring husband, beautiful boys, a successful career, financial comfort, and a lovely home. Who could ask for anything more?

Me. *I* was asking for more. And I felt guilty about it. I was never truly satisfied, and was always looking for gratification through some means—mostly shopping, eating, and drinking. Deep inside, I knew there was more to me and the life I was living—but I felt vulnerable and unsure of what I was actually looking for.

My perfect little present began to unwrap itself as my career progressed to a point that made me question everything about who I was and how I showed up in the world. I was forced into an organization that did not value my leadership skills—which, to me, meant that I wasn't valued as a person. Every day, I had to check my emotions and vulnerability at the door. My light was being smothered, but I felt like I had no other choice. I either had to go against my values to fit in, or take a risk—but I was not a natural risk-taker. I was always trying to do the "right" thing in order to avoid rejection and keep others from seeing me the way I saw myself: as someone who wasn't really good enough.

I hid my "not good enough" thinking by doing everything possible for others, no matter where I was—at home, at work, or in the community—and then proclaiming that this self-sacrifice made me happy. But after months of stress and tension, I finally had to ask myself, "*Why* do I believe that acting this way makes me happy?"

Honestly, I had no answer. I just knew that, despite what I was telling everyone around me, I wasn't happy. My life didn't seem to fit the real me.

Except, I had no idea who the real me was, or what her ideal life would look like.

My career gave me my first wake-up call. Over the years, it had become my life. Despite the fact that I couldn't show up authentically, I burned with the need to show my bosses and peers that I was "good enough." This unrelenting drive was a constant source of stress, but I was able to ignore it until it physically impacted me.

In 2013, I went for my annual mammogram appointment. They found a suspicious spot and biopsied it, citing two potential outcomes: cancer, or a pre-cancerous condition known as a radial scar. Given that my mom is a two-time breast cancer survivor, the doctor assumed the worst.

I swore that my priorities would change, and that I would no longer let work define me. "Please, God," I begged. "Just let me be okay!"

Although I didn't understand it at the time, my angels were with me. The biopsy determined that the spot was a radial scar; I would need surgery to remove it. As I prepared for the procedure, I asked my surgeon what caused radial scars.

"Stress," he said. "Are you under any?"

My answer was an immediate, "Yes!"

In that moment, I knew that my choices were creating more stress than my body could handle. I needed to wake up to the fact that my career didn't fit my values, my priorities, or my vision for my life. In fact, it was slowly destroying me.

My successful career began to look ugly to me. It became an ordeal to drag myself into the office. I was forced to produce results the old-fashioned way, without regard to the needs of my employees, when what I actually wanted to do was work with my employees to realize their dreams. Those meetings and financial strategies and planning sessions I'd pretended to love now felt suffocating. Was this really what I wanted to be doing for the next twenty years of my life?

I was afraid to answer my own question. And so, I gave up.

I gave up on my career, and was left floating somewhere between

"I don't care" and "I'm not good enough." I gave up on my self-care, gained weight, and felt even more self-loathing than before. I floundered in the endless sea of everyone else's expectations, far from any shore I could see. As a perfectionist, I wanted—no, *needed*—to be everything to everyone ...

Everyone, of course, except myself.

I needed to take back control of my life, and discover what I was really here to do. I made a promise to myself that I would reconnect with who I was; that I would "go home" to my core, and reawaken the person who was longing to come out.

And, for the first time in my life, I gave myself permission not to be perfect.

I had lost sight of my priorities, I realized. It was time, now, to clearly define and own them. I asked myself, "What makes me fire on all cylinders?" The answer: when I used my creativity and passion to inspire transformation in others.

It was that realization that directed me towards becoming a life coach. I found a Pinterest post advertising a certification program, which felt like a sign from the Universe—and suddenly, all of my old doubts and fears came rushing back to keep me stuck. Did I really want to spend the money on this? What if I wasn't good enough? My husband, understanding, encouraged me to take the chance on *me*.

I enrolled—and immediately realized that everything I was "learning" from the course, I had already cultivated through life experiences and my leadership role at work. I remembered how much I loved helping my employees create breakthroughs; I had been coaching them without realizing what I was doing! Waves of relief washed over me. My fears, doubts, and insecurities dissolved as I realized that *this* was my awakening. My purpose was born.

The next sign I received was an invitation to listen to a presentation by a success and purpose coach. What I learned from that talk changed my life. From that moment on, I swore that I would no longer accept drifting as a form of living.

And so, I made a huge decision, and quit my corporate job. So much for not being a risk-taker! I gave up my nice salary and benefits, and instead took action on my top three priorities: being home with my boys after school, working from home, and helping others as an entrepreneur. In just a few short months, I had accomplished it all. Through trust and faith, in my support group and myself, I had made it happen.

The best part of my perfect present, though, still lay unwrapped. I still had to clean out my "inner home." Working with my coach, I realized that I needed to learn forgiveness, understand gratitude in its real form, release my fears, and walk in my power: only then would I be free from the perfectionism and people-pleasing that had taken over my life. I found this release through my daily practices of self-discovery and reconnection with my spiritual center. I spent weeks writing letters to myself and to others, saying the things that needed to be said before I could move on with my life. I did clearing exercises, and sought the help of my Inner Light Healer to remove energy blocks. I connected with my intuition through meditation and quiet reflection.

When I truly began to practice gratitude—rather than just gratification—I began to see with new eyes. I saw how I have enough, how I *am* enough.

Now, I see grace as the ability to both give and receive. It's something I never truly understood before.

During one of my meditations, I met my guardian angels: Joy, Maggie, and Mary Francis. This magical experience restored my faith, and renewed my trust that I am taken care of and divinely loved. Not long after, God sent me a dream. My husband and I had been granted the ability to fly, and as we soared over a forest, I exclaimed, "Look at the beauty in these trees! My heart is *so* open right now to receive!" Then, I heard His words. "You are here to serve me and do my work." Can you imagine? I never could have received these experiences without opening my heart to gratitude and grace.

I have my answer. I am on the path I was always meant to discover. I am no longer adrift; instead, I'm swimming strongly through the ocean's currents, never far from my home.

What does the word "perfectionist" mean to you?

_____

_____

_____

_____

Where in your life are you trying to "be something"? What do you think would happen if you stopped trying to meet that ideal?

_____

_____

_____

_____

When have you experienced deep inner connection? What did that experience teach you about yourself?

_____

187

_____

_____

_____

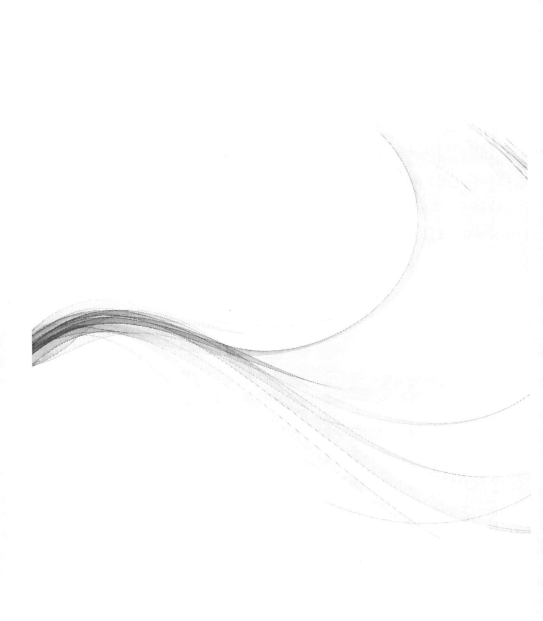

A Gateway for Love

Shelley Lundquist

I lay restlessly, awaiting the Sandman's arrival whilst Earth's dark, umbral shadow kissed a passionate farewell to his lover, Luna, on the other side of the world.

I heard it, before I saw her—the lovely lure of her tranquil song.

When I opened my eyes, there she was, peering patiently down at me through the window pane, her flawless face smiling as she beckoned. I gratefully accepted her invitation, emerging from the shadows of my home to join her on her peaceful playground. I trusted her implicitly.

My breath caught at the beauty of the backdrop before me. It was as though I'd walked into the page of a pop-up book and into my very own fairy tale. Luna was a perfect pearl hung high upon the sky, set elegantly amongst her celestial sisters and brothers. On one side, sliding nonchalantly down the handle of the Big Dipper, was noble Arcturus in his dazzling light. Just above, on her other side, golden Saturn gleamed with pride, his hula-hooping skills second to none. I felt at home amongst old friends.

But it was she—Luna, in her milky iridescence—who held my attention. I peered up at this opalescent beauty in rapture as the tendrils of her moonbeams reached down to embrace me.

As she held me, she whispered softly, "Let go. Release everything with unconditional love." And so, I did.

Her light filled me, illuminating every cell of my body. I felt the teardrops fall over my face, and her smile as she kissed them away. The night air, fragrant with the intoxicating scent of magnolia blossoms, left me heady; as I breathed it in, its soothing essence cleansed my mind, body, and spirit.

I was free.

Luna kept me company as I walked for a while, my steps ever so much lighter than they had been before. I smiled, flattered, as the night wind danced around us, whistling and flirting. Standing on the bridge which connected the park to the deserted schoolyard, I saluted the ever-vigilant basketball nets where they stood erect and on guard. The babbling of the brook beneath was positively jubilant, and the trees rustled their branches to get my attention as one last Lyrid meteor winked on its way by.

When at last I stood in front of my house again, Luna and I beamed at each other. I silently thanked her and bid her good night—but she held me there, her message incomplete. Uncertain, I waited as she bade me look.

From the West it came, racing across the sky. I watched, transfixed, as the cloud formation neared, and a dark shape took form as the wolf spirit burst from the billows as eyes the color of liquid honey met my astonished gaze—and then, the most amazing thing happened.

As I stood there, I felt myself grow. Taller and taller. Higher and higher. Higher than the moon, until I was so big that I disappeared into everything.

I knew, in that moment, that it is of this "everything" that I am made. The whole Universe is within me; as it is, within us all.

"*You're ready,*" I heard. "*Accept your gifts. Do not be afraid.*"

And then, suddenly, the clouds were gone, and Luna was moving away. I stood there, naked with the truth. *I am one with all that is.*

When we are open and truly present, we don't just witness the beauty around us: we become it.

I slept deeply that night, my dreams vivid. I awakened refreshed and with a profound sense of clarity, flowing with gratitude that I finally knew what I needed to do. In that moment of divine grace, I had heard the message loud and clear. I had to get out of my own way.

Despite convincing performances to the contrary, I'd been a loner most of my life, skirting the periphery of belonging with self-imposed reclusion. Nevertheless, I'd always had an innate ability to understand and connect with people, and to sense the truth behind their words and actions. My willingness to be vulnerable inspires others to open to me. When energetically strong, I had a lot to give, and willingly became what I felt others needed me to be. But time and time again, I discovered that sacrificing myself always rankled—and as my resentment rose to the surface, I eventually drifted away from the people I'd once embraced.

When out of balance, I struggled to be around people while coping with sudden energy shifts and the ravaging physical and emotional effects of bearing others' intense emotions. For a long time, being an empath seemed more like a curse than a gift. I was an angst-sucking sponge and, when crammed to the pores with everyone else's negative emotions, I needed to release that toxic cloud or succumb to it.

For many years, I did not manage this release well—and those closest to me bore the brunt. Professionally, I would compartmentalize to cope, as suppression was the only way I knew how to manage. Outside of work, I took everything personally, and would sometimes blow a gasket over little things that, on other days, would not faze me at all. I named this part of me Petula, the petulant one.

Petula was reactive, short-tempered, uncompassionate, and occasionally cruel. I was not proud that she was a part of me. My inability to control my emotions shamed and inflamed me, triggering a desire for retreat. It was fight or flight, and self-imposed seclusion seemed the kindest choice. It was a very lonely path.

Once, Petula snapped at my daughter before I could stop her, and my daughter fled to her room in tears. Filled with immediate remorse, I went to her side and hugged her tight. "If I ever lose my temper again," I told her, "remind me that you are just a little girl." I knew this counter-measure would defuse me immediately, and send Petula packing.

Thankfully, the Universe always sends us what we need. Over time, Nature became my teacher and my sanctuary. With her guidance, I learned to pay attention, navigate obstacles, and open to an inner journey. Her flowers taught me to turn my face to the sun, and let the shadows fall behind me. Her reeds taught me the importance of flexibility, and of bending in a storm. Her trees taught me how to stand tall, and to be resilient. And, perhaps most importantly, she showed me the peaceful harmony in the interconnectedness of all living things. It was here in Nature's loving arms that I first learned to quiet my mind and be fully present. I became aware that in stillness, I am the watcher of my thoughts, and can create space for emotions to flow through me and disappear. Here, I can bring myself back to a place of peace and lightness.

The first time I felt Petula approach after my outing with Luna, I was with my son. Instead of arguing with him, I stepped back, let go of emotion, and responded with love. In letting go of judgment, I was astonished at how everything shifted. I'd never before realized that judgment is as much a choice as compassion.

With my heart split wide open, I learned to love those parts of me that I had once hated—including Petula. I knew now that she was there to point me in the direction I needed to grow. Learning to understand the reason for her being, and finding compassion for her, ultimately led to her auspicious departure.

The healing that comes with self-acceptance rippled through my life. As I embraced my carefree nature, I began living from my truth, and watched as the pure expression of who I am and the love I bring to the world illuminated my life. I saw clearly that struggle ends when we are in harmony with ourselves—*all* parts of ourselves.

While spending time alone is still part of my sacred self-care, it no longer feels like hiding. Now, my solitude recharges and empowers me to open and share my gifts with the world. My daily walks and morning meditations keep me grounded in love, and allow the wisdom of the Universe to flow to and through me. My feelings of loneliness have vanished, as I am no longer focused on separation.

Finally, I have learned to open and share my own struggle instead of trying to manage on my own. I flourish in relationships that are nourished by understanding, kindness, compassion, and empathy. When I feel someone hurting, instead of being overwhelmed by their emotions, I pause, center myself, and open my heart wider. I become the watcher who feels beyond the suffering to see the light within each person. For all our differences, we are all the same. We want to be seen, be heard, and know that we matter.

With empathy, every relationship becomes a mirror of the Self, and a beautiful gateway for love.

How often do you allow yourself to experience beauty?

_____

_____

_____

_____

Shelley was called to step into her gifts, and not be afraid. Where are you avoiding your gifts, purpose, or passion? What would happen if you owned your gifts fully?

_____

_____

_____

_____

Shelley felt, during her experience, that she was "one with all that is." How do you see yourself as connected to the rest of life?

_____

_____

_____

_____

Naked in Public

Tonya Melendez

"You can never judge a book by its cover" is one of my all-time favorite quotes. It explains what is within us. The cover of a book is what gets it off the shelf and into your hands, but it's the words within that cast a spell.

We all have a story lurking inside of us. If we don't like that story, we often put on a mask, a cover, to protect ourselves from the world. But underneath this mask, this shield—this book cover—lies our Soul, our multifaceted and multilayered essence.

Once the Soul is allowed to reveal its radiance, light is reclaimed— but that allowing requires us to open the cover, set aside the mask, and unwrap the layers which keep us hidden away.

In other words, in order to reveal ourselves and stand in our essence, we have to get naked.

Stripped

For many years, I'd dreamed of living a fairy-tale life in Europe. Then, I did it, more than once … And I still wasn't happy. Sitting in the hookah lounge of an exclusive club in Spain, I found myself dreaming of the life I wished I had, instead of loving the life I was living. I kept waiting for "the good stuff" to happen.

All my life, I'd been living in the shadow of my stories. I could tell you those stories now. I could tell you the story of the emotional and sexual abuse I endured in early childhood; or share the tales of "I can't" and "I don't have" that I fed myself as a young single mother. I could tell you about my life as a librarian, or how I made a living

195

cleaning toilets in Key West before being whisked off to become a European TV star and the number-three psychic in the world. But I won't. I don't want to go back in time, because I'm moving forward; those stories no longer define me.

Not long after that night in the hookah lounge, I was awakened by a Voice. *"A void has been created,"* it told me. *"You must return to the United States and commit to your gifts."*

It was a call for the total surrender of my stories, and who I thought I was. Not only did I need to surrender the negative stories, I needed to surrender my successes, my rank, and my identification with my ego.

I couldn't lie or hide myself anymore. My Soul wanted me to bare it all, to strip away anything that kept its radiance hidden. I needed to allow who I claimed to be—who I prayed to become—to emerge, once and for all.

It wasn't a question: I had to listen to the Voice. All I could do was forgive myself for the mistakes I'd made, release my fears, and accept the next step with gratitude and grace.

Exposed

Back in the United States, I began the process of reinventing myself. I hadn't realized that my feelings of unworthiness led me to play small. I was constantly sabotaging myself, giving up or trying something new before I could be successful at what I'd started. More, I made excuses for behaviors that limited my growth.

I believed that, because I was a "good" spiritual person who prayed and meditated daily, gave to charities, and tithed to my church, it wasn't problem for me to indulge in a few ciders each night. I mean, even Jesus drank wine, right?

But it *was* a problem. I had a level of success as a psychic that was enjoyable, but my heart kept telling me that I had more to give, share, discover, do, and be.

I ignored those messages for a long time. I didn't know what it was like not to drink, or who I would be if I didn't have that escape. And so, I kept drinking—but every time I picked up a bottle, I got new messages from my Soul, telling me that there was more for me on the other side of this addiction.

When I finally quit, I stopped cold turkey.

Stripped of the comfort of alcohol, I didn't know what to do. I didn't know who I was. The stories I'd told myself about who I was had scared me into believing I wasn't worthy of what my Soul desired.

Never in my life had I felt worthy. My cover—the brave face I'd been presenting to the world—was a lie.

On my knees, through the tears, I bared my Soul, and asked to be freed. I asked that my freedom be effortless, that my intuitive channel would expand to include not just those I served as a psychic, but myself as well.

I craved to know what it would be like to be fully committed to my Soul and spiritual practice all the time. I craved to know what it would be like to be "happy" in the way that all the great spiritual teachers talked about.

Naked

One morning, it occurred to me that I had stopped counting the days I'd been free of alcohol. Something was different. *I* was different.

Now that I was paying attention, I was amazed at how clear my senses were. Alcohol had dulled my perception, but now I was experiencing all of life—both spiritual and mundane—as if for the first time.

My mask had been removed, my cover blown. I was showing up as totally raw and real, opening my personal book for the world to see. Turns out, what was written on the pages of my book wasn't what I thought it would be. I wasn't crazy, cursed, or helpless. I wasn't even all that weird. I just had a few flaws and screw-ups like everybody else.

Now, standing in my own skin and with my Soul shining brightly, I'm claiming opportunities for myself that I would have once considered beyond my reach. Giving myself permission to shine allowed those old stories to be rewritten, and years of pain to be dissolved. Had I still been drinking, or wearing my many masks, I might have missed many of my most treasured experiences—like traveling to New York City to do a live Periscope Tarot reading with Kimra Luna, working with Selena Soo to "Impact Millions," or writing the chapter you're reading right now.

"Be who God meant you to be, and you will set the world on fire," wrote St. Catherine of Siena. Denying my worth kept me on the shelf and in the dark for most of my life. Leaning into Spirit and my own Soul allowed my unworthiness to heal and my true radiance to reveal itself.

Now, I'm naked in public, sharing my gifts and the treasure of my Soul with everyone I meet.

Reflection

Tonya writes, "All my life, I'd been living in the shadow of my stories."
What stories about your past overshadow your current self?

....

....

....

....

What behaviors do you engage in that limit your growth? What excuses
do you make for these habits—and what would happen if you stopped
making them?

....

....

....

....

What would it feel like to be "naked in public," as Tonya describes?
What shame or stories could you release if you simply bared it all?

....

....

....

....

On Top of the World

Bev Janisch

After spending ten long days hiking and nine cold nights sleeping in a tent, I made it to the top of one of the highest mountains in the world, Mount Kilimanjaro in Africa. As I stood on top of the world, tears running down my face, I had a profound sense of inner excitement for having achieved something that I didn't know would be possible.

I decided to climb Mount Kilimanjaro for my fiftieth birthday because I needed a challenge in my life. I also knew that something was missing, and I had a deep desire to "figure it out." I had a romantic idea that the answer I was looking for would magically be found on the mountain.

Boy, was I wrong!

What happened next surprised me. After the initial exhilaration of reaching the top wore off, I felt as low and as empty as I ever had in my entire life. I returned home after this huge accomplishment with a heavy heart and a dull inner ache.

A few years before my mountain climbing adventure, I had retired relatively young from a long and fulfilling career as a nurse. My husband Mark and I were living the dream. We traveled to exotic places, spent time with amazing family and friends, and were splitting our time between vacation homes. The icing on the cake of my "perfect" life was that Mark was my high school sweetheart; we had been together for over thirty years.

With so much to feel grateful for, it was no wonder that my unhappiness and discontent were so confusing to me. I felt lost and alone, and couldn't put my finger on what was missing in my life. I

201

had so much—was I selfish for wanting more?

"Something must be seriously wrong with me," I thought. "Why can't I just be happy?"

I felt like I was going through the motions. I tried to put on a happy face and hoped that I would snap out of whatever was going on. But I didn't; it only got worse. Something in my life needed to change; I just didn't know what it was.

A few months after the Mount Kilimanjaro climb, I sat Mark down and said, "I don't know what's wrong with me, but I need to go back to our home in Canada and have some space to figure it out."

We were both scared and uncertain, not knowing what this really meant. As I write this now, I have tears in my eyes, and my heart aches remembering how confused we both were.

Within a few days, I was on a plane, heading back to my empty house in Canada in the middle of winter. I had no idea what I was going to do there, or even why I needed to be alone. I just knew that I needed time and space to reconnect with my soul and find myself.

For the next few months, I went into a cocoon. I had always been an extrovert, so this was quite shocking to me. All I wanted to do was spend time alone. I read, walked, and just spent time finding my own rhythm—one that wasn't based on other people's expectations and needs.

This was the beginning of my transformation. It was a painful and confusing time, but the pain was mixed with hope. I had no idea what it would look like when I came out; I just knew that I was grateful for the space to consider the inner turmoil that was still screaming, "*Something* needs to change."

While in my cocoon I began exploring my spiritual beliefs and started a daily meditation practice. For the first time in my life I went on an inner journey. I read countless books, journaled, began a gratitude practice, practiced forgiveness, prayed, and attended classes about anything and everything that would help me connect with myself.

As I began to reconnect with myself, I realized that I had always put my own needs second. No one asked that of me. There was a subconscious belief running my life: I thought I was here to support and help others, so I went along, didn't rock the boat, and made it work. This often meant putting my own feelings aside. I was a wife, mother, friend, sister, daughter, and devoted employee—but somewhere along the way, I lost my desires, and myself.

One of my most amazing moments of gratitude happened when I read *You Can Heal Your Life* by Louise Hay. She says, "If we are all responsible for everything in our lives, then there is no one to blame." That was a lightbulb moment for me. I realized that, without even realizing it, I had been blaming my husband for my unsettled feelings. I often thought, "If he'd just do this, or not do that, then I'd be happy." I had been giving away responsibility for my life without even realizing it.

Once I started "owning" my own life—my thoughts, feelings, and how I was spending my time—everything shifted. Whenever I started to focus on what others were and weren't doing, I'd say to myself, "Keep your hands in your own pockets." I realized that being focused on others was preventing me from doing my own work.

Another result of becoming more mindful was that I was able to feel just as grateful for the difficult emotions like loneliness, anger, frustration, and sadness as I was for the pleasant feelings of contentment, joy, and happiness. I started to feel *all* of my feelings, not just the "good" ones, and viewed everything as an opportunity to learn and grow.

The combination of gratitude and responsibility opened me up to grace. I became connected with my divine purpose, which is to heal, become whole, and mentor other women who are courageous enough to step fully into who they're meant to be.

I knew I was healing when I felt the inner shift from worry and anxiety to peacefulness and acceptance. As I healed from the inside out, I also healed my relationship with my husband. I no longer needed or expected him to "complete" me, because I was already whole. I knew who I was, what my desires were, and how to love myself.

When I emerged from my cocoon, a whole new world was waiting for me. It was like when Dorothy leaves her black and white world in *The Wizard of Oz* and sees a world in color for the first time. This new world felt peaceful, and full of wisdom and meaning. Gratitude no longer felt like something I *should* feel, or a mere thought; now, it was always in my heart, a new way of living.

When I had fully reemerged, miracles started to happen. I started to take baby steps towards the nudges from my soul. One step led to the next, and doors began opening as I followed my heart.

As I followed my inner guidance, the people around me began to heal themselves as well. I experienced the miracle of forgiveness, and of letting go of the need to control everything. I felt lighter as I let loose anger, resentment, and the heaviness of carrying around baggage from the past. My desire to serve others, which had once drained me, began to flourish.

I began to trust that I didn't need to have it all figured out before taking the steps; I just needed to *begin*, and trust my intuition. Out of that trust, my company, The Compassionate Mind, was born.

For the first time in my life I feel whole. I have emerged from my cocoon as a butterfly, deeply alive and passionate. My inner light and sparkle have returned. My days are filled with activities that are deeply meaningful, and relationships that are nourishing. I am grateful to live each day with the purpose and meaning that comes through living in a state of gratitude and grace.

Reflection

Have you ever accomplished something enormous, only to feel let down afterwards? Why do you think you felt that way?

_____

_____

_____

_____

Bev needed to retreat in order to find the way to gratitude and grace. How can you give yourself some "retreat time" in order to listen to your inner wisdom?

_____

_____

_____

_____

Bev writes, "I didn't need to have it all figured out before taking the steps; I just needed to begin." What can you do today, right now, to create the life you really want?

_____

205

_____

_____

_____

Transformed By Grace

Dr. Taura L. Barr, PhD, RN, FAHA

*O*ver the course of the last three years, I have completely transformed my life—mind, body, and spirit.

This wasn't by choice—at least, not at first.

My young adult years were a blur. I spent the majority of my time building my career. This meant long hours, working on weekends, and countless sleepless nights spent worrying about things that I now recognize are trivial. My husband and I did manage to have a family, primarily because he decided to stay home with our children to support my career aspirations. I thought that my husband's decision, and his generosity in making it, would make me happy—and it did, on the surface. But I wasn't thriving like I wanted to be. I was just *going*, running blindly with my nose to the grindstone, trying to be everything to everyone while not really being anything at all.

I probably would've kept this up for years if it wasn't for the fact that on February 23, 2013, I almost died.

The day started out like any other day. I was twelve weeks pregnant with my fourth child, and had just returned from a week-long trip out west. I was tired (since, once again, I couldn't sleep the night before), and had a headache, but since this was how I normally felt, I ignored it. I had to get to Washington DC to review grant proposals; I couldn't be bothered with a little pain.

As the day went on, though, my symptoms worsened to the point where I was having trouble breathing. I felt anxious and dizzy, like I was going to pass out. Then, I started spitting up blood.

I'm an intensive care unit nurse. When patients start spitting up blood, it usually doesn't end well. While I was accomplished at ignoring my daily aches and pains, this was something different, and it finally jolted me into action.

The feeling I had as my husband rushed me to the hospital is indescribable. It was like I was in another world. I knew exactly what was happening to me, yet I had no idea what was going on.

The next few days are fuzzy, but I remember a lot of pain, fear, and despair. After we arrived at the hospital, we quickly discovered that I had a blood clot lodged in my lung. It had likely been there for days—and, because I had not paid attention to it, it killed part of my lung. My lung began to bleed, which in turn placed a lot of stress on my heart, causing it to fail.

Even now, my heart races when I think about what might have happened to me and my baby. I could have lost my child and my life because I was too busy "being busy" to pay attention to my own health.

That first night in the hospital, I was in so much pain I couldn't breathe, let alone sleep. I had a pocket Bible in my purse that I hadn't opened in a while. My fingers landed on Psalm 22. "*My God, my God, why have you forsaken me?*" I read that passage over and over again until it hit me. God hadn't forsaken me; He was trying to wake me up! He had been trying to get my attention for a long time, and I hadn't been listening. In fact, I'd been ignoring Him so stubbornly that it took a near-death experience to get through to me.

Right then and there, I made a vow to myself and to God that I was going to take better care of myself so that I could use the gifts He gave me.

Since then, I've been in a process of transformation. I've had good and bad times, ups and downs, and everything in between. After my illness, I discovered that I carry a mutation in a gene that increases my body's ability to clot. This means I am at a much larger risk for heart attack and stroke than the general population, and this risk dramatically increases as I get older. Learning to live with this risk, and not be afraid of it, has been a large part of the new life and lifestyle I've created.

Health and wellness are gifts that we often take for granted. Most of the time, we don't even think about them until they are taken from us.

When I graduated from the University of Pittsburgh, I received a copy of Florence Nightingale's *Notes on Nursing,* which sat on my desk for years before I actually read it. Nightingale, the founder of modern nursing and a pioneer in the practice of wellness, believed in the ability of nature as the ultimate healer, and taught that patients were the best keepers of their care. Her practice emphasized the nurse as a vessel or conduit, someone who holds space for patients on their paths to wellness and empowers them to put themselves in a position where medical treatment will have optimal impact.

Being a vessel for my patients implies that I walk the journey with them as they discover their own paths to healing and wellness. I no longer feel the need to impose my beliefs and knowledge on those who are not ready or willing to accept them, or take charge of my patients' health without thinking about the consequences to my own well-being; rather, I meet patients where they are, and help them to find their inner strength and courage to take care of their own health as I now take care of mine.

As a nurse, I am a role model to my family, my patients, and the community at large. By living an intentionally well life, I actively seek wellness in all facets of my day, in all eight dimensions—physical, intellectual, social, emotional, spiritual, environmental, financial, and occupational. I'm learning how to put myself at the top of my own priority list, and how to stop worrying about things I cannot control.

Now, when I reflect on my illness, it feels like it happened to someone else. I don't feel like the same person I was three years ago. I'm healthier now than I've ever been. It was as if the old me died that day in the hospital, and the new, reborn me was the one who spent the next year gaining strength and learning to thrive. I was brought back to life with a new perspective. After spending ten years of my academic life studying ways to improve the diagnosis and care of heart disease and stroke patients, I have become my own patient, and that's a blessing.

Everything happens for a reason, even if sometimes those reasons are hard to see. There are messages all around us. Some, we see and

209

hear. Others, we feel. I have a deep connection to nature, particularly flowers, and I spend many hours caring for, drying, and pressing flowers to decorate my home. The spring after my illness was divine. I felt so alive as I readied my flower beds for the spring bloom. As I pulled out the prior year's foliage to make room for the new, I was struck by an overwhelming feeling that I was simultaneously cleaning out the old in me—that I was letting go of the things that were holding me back, and allowing the new growth within me to take hold.

Each struggle brings an opportunity to reinvent ourselves. With practice, we can open our hearts to the messages we receive every day, and allow our stories to unfold into the lives we are destined for.

For it is by grace you have been saved through faith—
and this is not from yourselves, it is the gift of God.
                                                    - Ephesians 2:8

Reflection

Are there messages coming to you that you've been ignoring? What do you feel would happen if you listened and responded to them?

_____

_____

_____

_____

Think of a time in your life where you experienced pain—either physical or emotional. What did you learn from this experience? How could you use this knowledge to gracefully meet similar experiences in the future?

_____

_____

_____

_____

Do any areas of wellness—emotional, financial, social, spiritual, occupational, physical, intellectual, or environmental—need attention in your life? What can you do to bring balance to these areas and create intentional wellness?

_____

211

_____

_____

_____

CHAPTER
Seven

Grace is ...
Feminine Connection

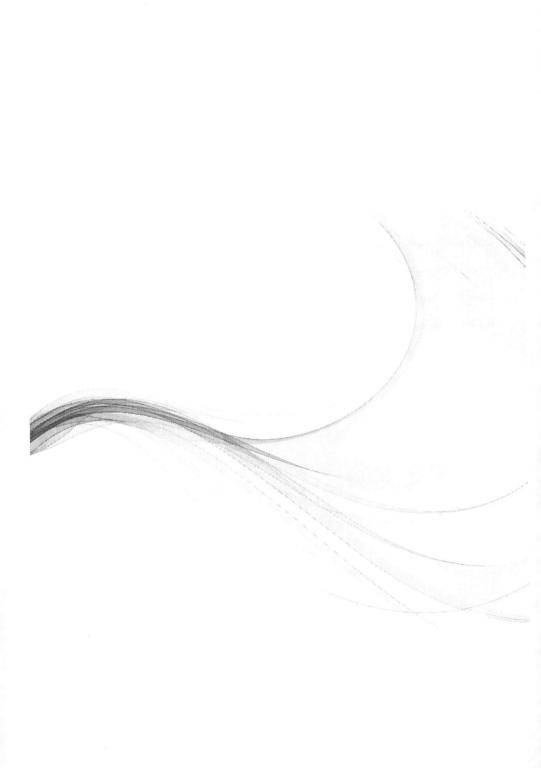

The Return of Shakti

Zinnia Gupte

"*G*ather the priestesses."

These three words shimmered over the cerulean waves as I meditated by the sea cave. It was a sacred calling.

I had been living on the Goddess Island of Ibiza, an ancient Mediterranean island in Spain. I was there to retreat and rejuvenate while healing from a divorce. I knew I had the medicine woman archetype deep inside my bones. I am from the Shakti lineage in India. My mother is Shakti. My aunt is Shakti. My grandmother, great-grandmother, great-great-grandmother—they were all priestesses of Shakti. The voice of India's ancient river flows through our bloodline.

Images flashed in front of me. I saw the women in my family performing their sacred feminine rituals of *Anjali* in the morning, and *Arati* in the evening. I saw my grandmother, freshly bathed, anointing herself in jasmine oil. With her wet, black hair, she stepped up to her altar: Goddess Kali was waiting, along with Dhurga, Lakshmi, and Saraswati. All the faces of Shakti. My grandmother lit incense and chanted sacred mantras to the paintings of the Goddesses. She rang a brass bell to clear the air. She offered flowers and a copper jar of water, and blew a white conch towards the sky.

My grandmother often took me to the temples of Kali, and to Dhakineshwar, a famous pilgrimage site along the River Ganges.

I held my grandmother's teachings close to my heart. However, growing up in the United States, I could not express these teachings to the wider world. The messages I received at school, from the men in my family, and on television, were very different from the feminine power of Shakti. I was taught to be ashamed of my body and my gifts from a young age. At school, I was laughed at, and humiliated in public by friends who thought I was "weird." Boyfriends rejected me, saying I was "too much" and "too intense." Family members constantly told me to cover my body. I began to believe that my beauty was dangerous, and that my voice didn't matter. I had an inner urge to step forward and be a powerful, visible, pioneering woman—but I believed that if I did so I would lose the love of my mother and father, as well as my closest relationships. And so, I stayed small. I didn't speak. I didn't express my power.

The voice rose from the ocean, calling me: "*Gather the priestesses.*"

For months, I healed through layers of victim mindset. I was a woman with little access to resources, no idea how to generate wealth, weak boundaries, and a sense of powerlessness over my life's purpose. I prayed every day to the spirit of the island to show me the way.

In September, I received an invitation to join a workshop for feminine magic. I had no idea what to expect. I was a practitioner of Tarot, had studied Hermetic and Egyptian texts, and had made pilgrimages to sacred Goddess sites around the world, but I had no idea what would be taught at this workshop. I went anyway.

The day of the gathering, the sun rose smiling through the East, and warm yellow light sparkled through my window. I bathed, and anointed myself with oils. I chanted the holy Shakti mantra and blessed the day.

One by one, the women arrived. We were in an old, Spanish-style building with mosaic floors, wide verandas, and green-shuttered windows. The workshop leader, Susannah, introduced herself and led us through the material. We sat in a circle, passing around sage, burning away unnecessary energy. By the time afternoon came, we were all bonding, chatting, and sharing stories with one another.

Later, we each drew a star: one triangle in gold to represent the male solar principle, and the other in silver to represent the female receptive principle. We were guided to write the qualities we most wanted to manifest in the next six to twelve months. I wrote "courage, wildness, abundance, instinct, and prosperity"—and then, I wrote "priestess" at the crown of the star.

Susannah took the paper in her hands and smiled as if she knew a secret. "You are meant to mentor young women, Beautiful One."

"Me?" My voice cracked. "What would I teach? Why would they listen to me?"

"Give it time. It will come to you."

After the workshop, I went home and placed the star on my altar. I lit a white candle every day for twenty-one days to complete the wish.

And I waited.

I started dancing on the island, teaching women how to unlock their bodies and flow with music and energy. I meditated every day. I wrote in my journal and channeled the voices coming to me— empowering, loving voices reminding me what power was and where true, authentic power came from. They asked, *"Are you willing to be powerful? Are you wiling to use your gifts, to be in your power? Can you see how to use your power and purpose in a meaningful way? Are you willing to shine your light?"*

One year later, I met Diana, a shamanic healer who also went by the name of White Horse Spirit. I was still in need of deep, soul-level healing, and she helped me open up to my shadows and the pain of betrayal, loss, uncertainty, and doubt. She helped me see where I had lost power and joy in my magical, sacred center: my womb. We worked together, shedding and healing, until I was gaining power and momentum in my life again.

In one of our healing sessions I asked, "Where do I belong? What is my purpose in life?" The channeling that came through expressed that Shakti would be a great guide for me. I also had to let go of my previous identity as a disempowered woman in order to step into my power for the entire world to see and cherish. I was being asked to accept my spiritual heritage and identity as a priestess and oracle, and as one who has deep wisdom to share with the world.

Diana said, "On this island, if you stand in your power and sing your truth, she will sing back to you."

I made Ibiza my temple.

For three years I danced and became a celebrant, anointing women's circles as well as sacred Equinox and Solstice days with

Shakti mantras, fire dances, and group rituals. I worked with women to bring Shakti into their lives through chanting, prayer, dance, and presence in their bodies. I even traveled to other Goddess islands along the Mediterranean like Santorini and Crete. Every year, I grew more able to hold space as a priestess. Every year I claimed my power. Then, there came a moment of shining grace.

Many women from the island circled up in sacred ceremony on Es Vedra, the Temple of Light, a magical and magnetic rock that shot out from the ocean. It was the island's sacred landmark. For me, it was a point of no return. Whatever I spoke out loud here, I would manifest. I prayed, *Mother, grant me your strength. You are the Earth who nurtured and nourished me. Through you all life is renewed. I pray you, Mother, shower me with your Divine Light. Please, let me be worthy. Thank you. I love you.*

I opened the circle with a fire dance, spinning and swirling and receiving visions. In my vision, a woman on a lion rode towards me, and stood so close I could feel her fiery breath on my face. The lion roared like thunder. I was electrified and shaken.

I kept dancing.

I saw my ancestors walk into the temple with red hibiscus in their hands. I heard them speak, "You are the one. This is your time. You are worthy."

I saw young women passing through the fire with small flames in their hands.

I saw the shackles which had bound me for all of my life fall to the ground.

I asked for women to be in their power. I asked for my own activation of power.

I asked for women to speak their truth. I asked that I could finally speak the truth.

In that moment I faced my power, and was unafraid. I was transformed. I began to believe in myself, and in the possibilities of spreading Shakti not only in Ibiza, but to the whole world.

That was the moment I chose myself, and stopped waiting for anyone else to choose me. I chose to become the greatest version of myself—and it was time to share my message with the world.

Eventually, I left Ibiza, and moved to New York City. There, I founded Shakti Priestess, and became a five-time best-selling author by sharing the stories of my Kundalini awakening with Shakti. My own book, *Messages of Shakti*, found a global audience and community. Soon I was holding sacred circles for women, hosting my own podcast, creating guided meditations, and teaching my signature system called Shakti Power.

By reclaiming my voice, vision, power, and truth, I stepped into my sacred feminine power as a spiritual leader and priestess.

The ritual on the cliffs, singing to Es Vedra, was a reflection of the woman I had become. In my journey from victim to vibrant, visionary woman, I had created a foundation of power, and no one could take that away from me ever again. In my heart, in my blood and bones, I heard drums beating, and women chanting all around me. I felt the rivers of ancient India flowing through me. The power and the sound grew louder and louder. As I danced and sang with my heart open to the sky, my voice burst into a fiery roar. Truth was calling, the Goddess was calling, women around the world aching to be heard were calling.

And all across the sky, a sacred voice was calling ...

Reflection

What is your feminine heritage? How do you honor your female ancestors in your daily life?

_____

_____

_____

_____

Zinnia went to the Goddess Island to heal. Where is your soul called? How can you make a pilgrimage to your healing place a reality?

_____

_____

_____

_____

Zinnia writes, "By reclaiming my voice, vision, power, and truth, I stepped into my sacred feminine power." What power is waiting for you? What steps can you take to reclaim it?

_____

_____

_____

_____

Six Months to Live

Karen Smith

*T*he look in the doctor's eyes alone told me that I should stand.

"You'll be lucky to be alive in six months," she said.

"*What?*"

"You have Hodgkin's disease." She spoke with her head tilted down slightly, eyes looking up at me. "Without immediate chemotherapy, you have about six months to live."

How had this happened to me?

At that time in my life, I was working twelve- to fourteen-hour days at my clothing store. I was traveling at least twice a month, chowing down on fast food every night because I lacked the energy to cook. I hardly saw my young daughter. I had no idea who my husband was anymore. I had no idea who I was anymore, either.

As a child, I'd spent a lot of time trying to control my chaotic world. My environment was so unstable that I constantly felt like I had to protect myself. I was the "strong firstborn," always looking out for my three younger siblings. Our house was not a safe place to share feelings, or be vulnerable. When the fights escalated to the point where things were being thrown, punched, and broken, I would get my younger siblings out of bed and take them out into the garden, where we had a play house. It was my job, I felt, to protect them and keep them safe from the chaos and violence in our house. Eventually the cops would come, and things would quiet down—at least for the night—but I was always anticipating the next explosion.

Most of what a child's mind perceives from a chaotic environment is unworthiness, a sense of always being at fault. Unfortunately, our minds are like sponges when we're young, and what we absorb as children keeps running our life well into our adulthood. At twenty-eight years old, I was still running my life in the same way I had as a child: armoring up, protecting myself and everyone else, achieving more and more, and above all establishing *order*.

For my whole life, I'd suppressed any painful or negative emotion, numbing out anything that might arise from within me, and splintering off parts of myself that didn't fit my ideal of perfection. Not only did this take away from my wholeness, but it made me unable to let love in. The most important parts of life, I was shutting out.

When I finally got into the college of my dreams, I got pregnant. Out of fear, I married a man I barely knew. In hindsight, I can see that I attracted the very type of disconnected relationship I had with myself.

What does all of this have to do with my Hodgkin's diagnosis? All of that unexpressed emotion was wreaking havoc in my body. I was using up all of my energy to keep my feelings shut away, and living in a constant state of fear, worry, and anxiety. All of the resources my body would normally use to heal and maintain itself were instead keeping me in a constant state of high alert. As a result, my immune system shut down.

I pushed through the tiredness and disconnection, and opened my first brick-and-mortar store, which became a huge financial success. More stores followed. And then, after three years in business, I felt the first lumps on my neck.

I ignored them, assuming it was an allergy. Weeks later, the bumps had spread, but they didn't hurt so I figure they would go away. As I shampooed my hair, I noticed that they were now in my scalp. Finally, I saw my doctor, who called in a personal favor to have a renowned oncologist see me immediately.

Now, after a three-hour examination, I was standing in her office, listening to her tell me I had six months to live.

"I don't think so!" I blurted.

The doctor stared at me, aghast. At last, she gasped, "Do you know who I am?" She then went to prattle on about her standing in the medical world, and her decades of work and achievements.

Again, without thinking, I said with conviction: "What does that have to do with me?"

I picked up all of my paperwork, and the manila envelope on her desk, and left. When I opened my file in the car, I saw that she had already prepared the prescription and instructions for what she described as "urgent, light chemotherapy."

I've felt the presence of angels. As a child, hiding in my darkened room while the fights and chaos raged outside, I've felt wings at my back, and butterflies in my stomach. I've always known, on some level, that there was something out there that was greater than me; something magical and powerful beyond what I could imagine. I did not know, then, that I was feeling the gentle presence of grace.

Coming home after my appointment with the oncologist, I walked into my living room—and there, sitting on my couch, was an angel.

The feeling that flushed through my body was not unlike what I'd experienced when I was younger, but it was one hundred times more powerful. This little angel, in the human form of my four-year-old daughter, looked at me with the biggest smile and widest, happiest eyes I've ever seen in my life. She ran up to me, squealing, "*Moooooommiiiiiieeeeee!*" like I have never heard before or since. Her tiny arms reached up to me and I grabbed her tight. Looking into those precious, gem-like eyes, my body shivered. In an instant, decades of guilt and shame were flushed out by the light of grace.

From that instant forward, all I focused on was how grateful I was for my precious child.

I never saw that oncologist again. I went to the bookstore and bought books on self-healing and quantum physics. I had never bought from the self-help section before, but I've always believed that "where there's a will, there's a way." I changed my diet immediately, and detoxed my body. I did not let other people's fears or doubts in.

No one, myself included, chooses to become sick. But daily, hourly, minute-by-minute, how we choose to feel affects our bodies. We are choosing in every moment, from a place of either love or fear. My new choices did not come from fearing death. They came from fully loving life.

I had a purpose, and not even the threat of death would stop me.

I called my regular doctor, who was about to travel, and shared with him that I had absolutely no intention of doing chemo, and that I did not accept the prognosis. He scheduled me for a biopsy in four weeks' time, when he returned. I had four weeks, then, to prove I could heal myself.

I learned to meditate in tiny amounts. I learned to be still again, I remembered that in the depths of despair there was a loving whisper, a place that knew more than what my eyes could see. I had not been still since I was a teenager; in constant motion, I had since lost all sense of self, all ability to listen. I was running so fast from my own hurt that I had forgotten what it felt like to enjoy or be grateful for anything.

I learned that my thoughts have a profound influence on my health and well-being. I alone can think my thoughts; I alone can change the way I feel. In my previous race to achieve more and gain outside approval, I never even thanked myself for a single accomplishment, let alone took time to feel gratitude for all the amazing things I already had.

I learned firsthand that focus and intention with strong positive emotions (like gratitude) have a way of smoothing out life's bumps. Literally. Opening my heart to grace reduced the density of the heavy thoughts and feelings I'd been running from for so long. As I was sinking into gratitude, my lumps were shrinking and disappearing.

Four weeks passed. My doctor returned, and I went for the biopsy. It came back benign. The doctors were baffled.

I was sent for more tests. No one could explain my miraculous healing. The last specialist I saw had this to say: "Ms. Smith, whatever you had is gone without a trace. We can't find anything—except that you are, in fact, pregnant!"

I named my second daughter Seanna, which means "God is gracious." Four months after her birth, I separated from my husband and joined the hero's world of single moms. Relationships, like so many of the physical aspects of my previous life, could no longer exist in my new state of being.

My daughters are now fifteen and twenty, and they are gems in the world. After living in Florida for years, I now live in the place I dreamed of for years: Boulder, Colorado, right at the feet of the mountains. Even better, I have an amazing partner with whom I can share deep vulnerability, love, and connection. My gratitude practice has done far more than heal my body; it has helped me connect with my soul's calling, live my purpose, and help others see that we all have the unlimited ability to create and align with our destiny.

Reflection

Karen got a wake-up call in her diagnosis. What was your wake-up call—and what changes did you make because of it?

_____

_____

_____

_____

Karen discovered that her thoughts and feelings have a profound influence on her health and well-being. How do your daily thought and feeling patterns serve your health and wellness?

_____

_____

_____

_____

Karen writes, "I had a purpose, and not even the threat of death would stop me." What do you feel you must accomplish in this life?

_____

_____

_____

Remembering My Birthright

Sara Turner

My two white cats stared out into their brand new garden with elongated necks. They looked at me with huge eyes, as if to ask, "Where has our old garden gone? Where are we now?"

I replied, "Don't you remember? I've been saying for several years now that we are moving to a new house in a new land, and that your garden there will be bigger and more magical than anything you have ever experienced before. The air will be pure; there will be peace and quiet; and you will be able to run, hunt, and play. You will be free to embrace the wildness of *you*, and return home at night to the warmth of the fire, your plate of food, and our love."

They watched me trustingly as I spoke, and then meowed once more, "Well, let us out then!"

"No, boys," I said. "I can't do that right now. But I promise, one day soon we'll open the doors and you will be free once more. For now, just trust us."

I, too, gazed with wonder at the view that now greeted us through all of our windows. Willows waved at me, reminding me to be flexible. Buzzards flew high in the sky, showing me the importance of knowing the larger picture of life. Peach blossoms gently opened on our new trees, unfolding my heart and soul to new possibilities. Somehow, we had arrived, and were now living our dream, the seed of which had been planted so many years ago. Virtually all the elements of our new life that we had outlined in lists and on vision boards were here, in this new house, and on this land. Words could not describe our gratitude.

It's hard to believe how different my life used to be. At one time, I was broke, and lived in a house on a busy road, surrounded by incessant noise and toxicity. I worked in a job that drained me, and inhabited a body that was flooded with anxiety day and night. I remember only too well the horror of having to ask family and friends for help putting food on the table or paying our bills. There were weeks when a few eggs would have to last us several meals, and when we would have to search the house for coins to take the bus. I remember once running out of sanitary napkins and being unable to afford to buy more. The shame was overpowering. Why, I wondered, was it so hard to have even the most basic necessities of life?

Looking back, I know that these moments were part of the process of remembering my birthright—happiness—and learning that I was enough. Yet, at the time, it was unbearably hard and lonely.

During my first flower essence practitioner training, our group met monthly to take flower essences together and share our experiences and insights. On one occasion, I received the drop of a particular essence into my mouth, and found myself taking a deep breath and closing my eyes. The energy of the drop merged with my adult energy system and my heart, accessing memories I'd tucked away long ago.

Instantly, I saw myself as a small child in the front garden of my family's home. It was a sunny summer day, and I was puttering around, fingers in the earth, speaking to the snails, insects and flowers. That was the pivotal moment when I negotiated my life plan with Nature, and She offered me the promise of Her love and support. My end of the deal was to spread Her message far and wide, out into the world.

My forty-something-year-old self remembered, in that moment, who she used to be, before life's trials made her forget. She remembered the pure light, love, and innocence that she was before she grew up, and how the kingdom of Nature was her friend and her home.

My heart opened as I remembered once more making perfume from rose petals and capturing wood beetles in a special pot—and feeling so terribly disappointed the next day when they had all gone. I remembered my childhood love of trees, and how it was so hard to let go of the part of me who loved to climb them. I remembered coming home on the first day of my monthly bleeding, and cringing when my mum said, "When are you going to grow up and be like other girls?

Don't you realize it is not the "done thing" to be climbing trees at your age?"

As I grew through my teenage years, I forgot even more who I really was. I retreated into myself and became painfully shy. I enjoyed studying, and showed little interest in boys and partying. Although I had friends, I often felt left out and confused by my feelings of being "different."

I broke family patterns by becoming the first in my family to go to university. I studied marketing, and spent five years living in Paris. Whereas other women in my family married and became mothers after finishing school, domestic bliss was the last thing on my mind. I worked in China, taught in Sweden, and traveled around the world.

It wasn't that I didn't want to be married or have children. It was just that it never crossed my mind as an option. There were just so many other, more exciting life paths to follow, and so many things that kept pulling me forward and away from what was "normal."

My dad died very unexpectedly when I was in my late twenties. I was plunged into the depths of despair and ill health, and at the same time implanted with the first seeds of grace in my life's journey. Dad's departure gifted me with the charge of my mother, who struggled with being "left alone" and who never really recovered from his passing. During those first dark days, somehow, the flowers found me.

It was a chance conversation with my hairdresser, who mentioned that she knew a flower essences practitioner who might be able to help me feel better. I followed the link and within months was feeling much more like myself. What followed was my total immersion in the world of flower essences. I wanted to learn everything I could about them— and as I re-learned the sacred gifts of Nature, life and hope returned to my heart.

I was beginning the long journey back to myself, but the difficult days were far from over. Deep anxiety plagued my life. I felt a deep terror of *being alive* which challenged my body so much that I ended up hospitalized. As part of my recovery I left my teaching job and placed myself into the love and care of my soul partner and friends and family—but this necessary choice plunged us into the clutches

229

of poverty. I didn't understand what was happening to me. I didn't understand why it felt so hard to live.

Time passed, and strands of light continued to seep back into my life. A Chinese acupuncturist's loving care and explanations of what was "really" happening to me comforted my heart and gave me hope for the future. My daughter, Gaia, remained in my womb for only twelve weeks, but her passage through me—one of the most tragic moments of my life—gave me another key to the door to my future. Despite everything, I began to believe that it was okay for me to be here; that I had a purpose to fulfill.

Through all of these moments, I continued to immerse myself in flower essences, becoming a qualified Practitioner in Flower and Vibrational Medicine. I began to tune in to the immense support of the flowers, the trees, and the crystal kingdom. I realized that I was not alone, and never had been; I had just forgotten where I'd come from. I founded my own training school for flower essence practitioners, and this work began to support my partner and me in ways we had never before experienced.

My partner and I had dreamed of a house in France. We wanted an extraordinary garden with a view, numerous trees, and homes for our nature allies. Now, having undergone the long journey back to myself, I am richly supported in body, mind, and spirit. Poverty and anxiety are things of the past. The more I remember my promise to Nature, the more She provides for me and for those I love.

As humans, we often forget that what we need can come in many different forms. My gift of grace has been opening to the love of those who love me, whether they are humans, animals, flowers, or trees.

There is a beautiful, pale-pink flowering quince tree in my garden now. I hear her whisper of how she holds a beautiful heart space of love and nurture for me, and I am so grateful. My cats will soon be lounging in her branches, and running at her feet. I will hear her sing in the twilight as my partner and I sit under the moon. These are the gifts of my birthright—the right to be as I am, and at one with Nature.

Reflection

Were you told as a child that you should be more like others? What did you hide away based on that advice?

_____

_____

_____

_____

Sara describes a journey back to herself. What would it take for you to live as the fullest expression of yourself?

_____

_____

_____

_____

Sara dreamed of a house in France—and she made that dream come true. What dreams have you cherished for years? What steps can you take right now to make them a reality?

_____

_____

_____

_____

Carbonated Holiness

Lore Raymond

When I was thirteen, my mom announced that our military family was leaving southern California.

I passionately protested. "You're kidding me, right? I can't finish eighth grade and graduate with my friends from St. Francis de Sales?"

"No, you can't," she replied. "Your dad's been promoted and we're moving to Offutt Air Force Base."

"Where's that?"

"Nebraska."

"*Nebraska*?"

Like a dropped bomb, my mom's announcement dismantled the happy, safe, and known world I'd intentionally created for six years. My teenage life was shrapnel.

The firstborn child of an Air Force family, my life travels started in Big Spring, Texas. My journey continued to Japan, Kansas, California—and then, of course, Nebraska—thanks to my dad and the United States Air Force. But now, neither mom's hugs, nor Tolkien's seminal words, "Not all who wander are lost," could soothe me.

I felt lost. There was no laughter.

Fast forward four years, to my senior year of high school, when a similar announcement came.

"What do you mean, I have to move my senior year?" I screeched through a waterfall of tears.

My mom replied soothingly, "Next month, your dad is returning from Vietnam. We're being transferred from Nebraska to Maryland. He's assigned to the Pentagon. You'll adjust because you always have, sweetie."

Yes, surprisingly, I *had* adjusted, and even thrived after the previous move from California to Nebraska. I had evidence to prove it, too: I was inducted into my high school's National Honor Society, elected class secretary for two years, and honored as the Pep Club's "Most School-Spirited Person."

What my parents didn't know is that thriving after this most recent move entailed surviving many a mean-girl morning. As I walked through the halls with my boyfriend, the whispers of the clique followed me—hushed snickers like, "Oh my! Can you believe she's so flat-chested? A pancake! What does he see in *her*? She's so stuck up!" They slathered me with the residue of their own jealousy. Sadly, I absorbed their corrosive energies. My self-worth began to erode, and my confidence evaporated. I constructed my Teflon defense: girls were vicious enemies, and not to be trusted. (Except for my best friends, Deborah Jean and Mary.) There was no laughter.

After Nebraska, Maryland felt like another planet. I was back to being the new girl again, an alien amongst the established groups and cliques. These senior high school girls knew the comfort and familiarity that many a sleepover engenders, and I wasn't a part of their history.

It wasn't long before my parents chirped, "So ... Where do you want to go to college?"

Moi? I thought. *You're asking me now? Really?*

This was no casual question. I could be the first Raymond to seek and earn a college degree since my English ancestors arrived in New Hampshire in 1658. As a seventeen-year-old who had already traveled thousands of miles, moved, wandered, and felt lost, I knew this was a life-changing question, and one which deserved my heart-felt answer.

Yet, after surviving and thriving through four years of mean-girl mornings and two significant military-family transfers, *I just didn't know.* There were too many choices, too many "shoulds." Suddenly, after so many years at the mercy of my dad's job, *I* was empowered to choose my destination. This empowerment felt like putting on pantyhose on a summer day—the question didn't fit, or feel comfortable.

For reasons I didn't understand at the time, my free-will choice was to attend Judson College, an all-women's school. Founded in 1838, a time when formal education for women was rare, it was located in Marion, Alabama (population: 5,000), so once again I'd be a foreigner: the Yankee from Maryland.

I didn't apply to dozens of colleges or universities, although I could have. Nor did I know that Judson's timeless values would embody not only the woman I sought to be then, but the woman, mother, sister, and friend I hope I have become. All I knew is that when the enrollment offer came, the invitation was accepted with no hesitation.

The fallout included comments like *"You?* You're going to a women's college?" and "You're boy-crazy. I can't believe you!" But they didn't see it the way I did. I'd been accepted at a *women's* college. I had been accepted into a 136-year-old clique! This felt happy, and oddly healing.

This was a chance to transform my issues with women by stepping into a deeper journey towards healing, wisdom, and spiritual growth. And, during my first semester, I embraced experiences with women that led to leadership roles in the safe learning cocoon I shared with four hundred sister students. I served on, and eventually chaired, the Social Committee; wrote for the college newspaper and yearbook; and danced with, and eventually co-chaired, the Terpsichorean dance team.

In my second semester, the corrosive, self-esteem-destroying chatter started creeping back into my thoughts. Although Judson had been my enthusiastic choice, painful speed bumps appeared with roommates and classmates. Doubts and questions showed up like stop lights. In addition, my suite mate was transferring; she'd had enough. I started to wonder, *Who am I to think I could do this? What am I doing here at a women's college? What would my parents say if I changed colleges after all this time and money?* The "shoulds" weighed heavy on me, like a wet woolen coat on an Alabama summer day.

235

My youthful feelings of powerlessness and overwhelm returned. I felt like I had no control over where I was, or why I was there. At the same time, tsunami-like waves of relentless courses, tests, papers, and life's uncertainties were sinking my sailboat of joyance.

But this time, it was different. This time, *I could choose.*

On a Thursday afternoon in spring, our dorm windows were wide open, and the air smelled like sweet magnolias and mowed grass. My new freshman friends Nan and Greta unexpectedly popped into the room. "Want to go for a ride with us, Lore? It's so pretty out. C'mon!"

I hesitated. All the "shoulds" flashed.

"Rhonda and April are coming, too. Let's go, y'all!"

It seemed like a simple decision: go, or don't go. But in that moment, I said "yes" to more than just a springtime drive. I said "YES!" to respecting and appreciating these women—and all the women in my life—and to *my* choices.

I wasn't going to transfer to another college. I was included in a very special sisterhood, one that I wanted to be part of forever. Girls and women weren't my vicious enemies anymore. I would see my choices through to the end, and graduate into the world from Judson College.

For one salubrious afternoon, five hopeful freshman friends piled into Nan's lemon-yellow convertible and cruised through Alabama's countryside. Along the way, we stopped many times to pick hundreds of daffodils. Free from tests and classes, we giggled, and our laughter—our "carbonated holiness" as Anne Lamott would say—filled the countryside and our hearts. Afterwards, the daffodils, symbols of hope, graced every vase, mug, glass, pitcher, and water bottle we could round up.

I was hopeful. We all were. The bright, sun-soaked daffodils seemed to live forever. They still decorated our dorm rooms two days later for the annual Dad's Day Weekend.

Oddly, we never went cruising again.

Fast forward forty-four years. I graduated cum laude with a double major in Romance Languages and Elementary Education in just two years and ten months. Many of the women from my Judson College journey still grace my life today. Sadly, Nan didn't live forever—cancer took our dear daffodil driver our senior year—but I see and connect with my other classmates often. Their sacred friendship reminds me how grateful I am that I said yes to the experience of "carbonated holiness" that Judson College and my sisters brought to my life.

How do you address changes in your physical space, such as moving to a new state, home, or job?

_____

_____

_____

_____

If you hold any negative energy around girls or women, how can you release it in order to experience greater peace and connection?

_____

_____

_____

_____

How do you include strangers and newcomers into your life?

_____

237

_____

_____

_____

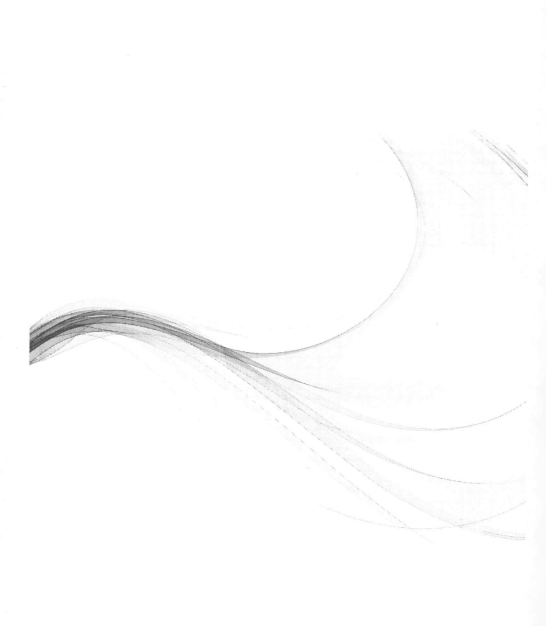

The Impossible Dream

Lisa Marie Rosati

"*B*e the change you want to see in your world."
I distinctly remember the electrifying jolt that hit me when I said those words to a private coaching client three years ago. Immediately after, I thought to myself, *Lisa, that's fantastic advice. Why don't you take some of your own coaching, and be the change you want to see in your world too?*

Whoa—what?

A hundred thoughts swirled in my head, and my heart pounded as I inquired within for guidance. Why was this particular message niggling at me? If I could just wave my magic wand, what would I change in my life? What would I want more of? What would I want less of? Could it be that the coaching which so easily rolled off my tongue for my client was meant for me, too?

And then, because I take my work very seriously, I instantly pushed away my thoughts and became present to my coaching session again. I vowed, however, to return to this cosmic message later that night.

The rest of my day progressed as my days usually do when I'm not traveling: coaching and marketing my business until late afternoon, then a quick hat switch to begin "mommy duties"—after school pickups and drop-offs, and cooking dinner. My boys were still young at the time, and my daughter was living in her own place, so I was the official taxi service of the Roth-Rosati household. I gave not a single thought to my earlier lighting jolt until I got in bed to begin my evening ritual of powering down.

I fluffed my pillows, laid my head down, and pulled my crisp white down comforter up over my legs and torso. Then, I closed my eyes, and asked the question:

What would I change in my life if I could?

What bubbled up to the surface surprised me. Suddenly, I was awash in memories of the times in my life I've felt betrayed or not taken care of by people I trusted. I thought I had already worked on and healed most of my wounds, however it was now very obvious that I still harbored massive pain and anger deep down. My jaw tightened, and my mood became foul as I journeyed into the dark place in my soul—the place that we magickal folk call The Underworld.

My past visits to The Underworld, and my meetings with the Dark Goddess, have never been easy or pleasant, but I have come to know that the only way to heal my wounds is to visit Her, and allow Her to guide me to the dark corners of my psyche where pain lingers and old wounds fester. So, down I went, right into the dark truth of my long-held pain, disappointment, betrayal, and anger.

I don't trust women.

Wow, I thought. *That's so sad.* But I wasn't really surprised. I'd secretly known this darkness to be my truth since my early school days, when I'd had such an excruciating experience at the hands of catty, mean-girl cliques. Until now, though, I'd never allowed myself to admit this.

Oh, no. *That* wouldn't be spiritual at all.

In order to protect my shameful secret, I came up with my go-to, lifelong excuse: that I am a lone wolf, and that it is in my nature to keep a healthy distance from others. It's not a charade: when I feel into my body, the lone wolf is most definitely my truth. However, I believe I evolved this way in order to survive the cruelty that life dished out. I just couldn't handle it, so I became a loner. Problem solved! (Or so I thought.)

I used that same lone-wolf cover for most of my adult life, too— right up until that day, three years ago, when I got hit in the head by that "be the change" cosmic 2x4. That night, as I visited the Dark Goddess from my bed, I finally decided I was ready to examine those old, deep-seated beliefs about my ability to engage in friendship and partnership with women.

I've been on a self-growth journey as a magickal practitioner for most of my life, so I knew that healing my feminine wound was going to be a process, not a quick fix. It had taken my entire lifetime to get to this wounded place; healing was bound to take time, too. There was a tremendous amount of pain and anger to identify and release, so a "quickie" was simply not going to happen. I remember feeling afraid to get started. The unknown has always been scary stuff for me.

"Lisa," I asked myself. "Do you really want to go there? Do you really want to open up this Pandora's Box?"

My first thought was, *Hell, no!* However, when I allowed myself to settle into the fear, I realized that my real answer was yes. Yes, I was ready. I didn't want to hold onto this pain any longer.

Long ago, I made a sacred vow that nothing and no one would ever get in the way of me being healthy and whole—and this feminine wound was holding me back from complete healing. Determined now, I got out of bed and stalked to my office, grabbed a pen, and—in my usual Creatrix fashion—dove into my journal.

What would my ideal relationships with women look like? I wrote.

The words started flowing. Truth be told, I was astonished by my response. I longed for a world where women gathered to discuss the things they loved and were passionate about. A world where women collaborated, supported each other, and held each other in times of need. A world where they celebrated the good stuff without jealousy, and helped each other succeed in business and in life because it gave rise to the world in the process. A world where they loved each other unconditionally, and never judged each other's actions or past.

After a while, I realized that my hand was cramping, so I took a break to read what I had written. My heart felt full. There it was, right in front of me. The world I dreamed of was a world of Sisterhood.

In that moment, it felt like an impossible dream. I cried the most compassionate of tears for the little girl inside me who would never feel like she belonged. I longed to be part of a tribe of kindred spirits that I could count on. I still remember the taste of those tender tears as they streamed down my cheek and into the crook of my mouth: warm, salty, and innocent.

Shortly after, Big Mike came home from work and asked why I was crying. (Crying is not a common occurrence in our home.) I only told him that some painful memories had come up, and asked him to hold me. He did, and we went to sleep.

While I slept, some divine guidance came through. I don't recall the exact message, but it carried the spirit of hope within the words. I had already known I would find a way around this, as staying in a place of "impossible" simply isn't in my nature. A pit bull in lipstick: that's me. And, because I heal my wounds through my work, I decided that the best way for me to "be the change" I wanted in my life was to create my very own Sisterhood.

The definition of "sisterhood" is a group of women linked by a common interest, religion, or trade, so I decided to create a virtual space that would attract women who were interested in the topics dearest to my heart: magickal living, ritual, manifestation, natural healing, and other esoteric subjects. It felt simple, natural, and yet totally overwhelming.

On launch day, I was out of town on a business retreat, and my assistant called to let me know that the payment process had a glitch. "I think we should push back the launch date until we figure this out," she said. I agreed, but felt so deflated. A little part of my mind said, "Lisa, I told you this whole thing was a bad idea."

I sulked the entire day, but the next morning I woke up more determined than ever to put this offering out there into the world. I got on the phone with my assistant and set a new game plan in motion.

One week later, technology snafu behind us, the Sisterhood's birth day finally came. I was beyond nervous: tingles everywhere, and nausea galore. As enrollments began to come in, I placed my hands over my heart and thanked the Almighty for the immediate affirmation. I had never imagined that there would be so many women out there who felt just like me: unable to fit in, betrayed by their own kind.

I was reborn the day my Sisterhood was birthed, and my sacred circle of beautiful, wise women has become my favorite place on Earth. Before that cosmic lightning strike, I would never have believed that courageously moving *towards* other women, with vulnerability and an open heart, would heal my deepest feminine wound.

Reflection

What are your deepest beliefs about women? How do they impact your daily life and relationships?

_____

_____

_____

_____

What would it take for you to heal your deepest feminine wound?

_____

_____

_____

_____

What steps can you take today to "be the change" you want to see in your own life?

_____

243

_____

_____

_____

Editor's Note

Bryna René Haynes

I'm so grateful to have had the chance to participate in the creation of the book. There is truly nothing more fulfilling for me than coaching inspired women through the process of writing and sharing their personal stories.

The alchemy which occurs during the process of writing the kinds of authentic stories you've read in this book is magical. The deceptively simple act of putting words on paper can transform both writer and reader, and take both to a new level of understanding and connection.

That understanding and connection permeates every page of this collaborative book. The very nature of grace requires this level of intimacy—this willingness to let down our walls and drop our veils, and be seen the way the divine sees us. Every one of the authors in this book has done that for you, reader, so that you may see, feel, and *know* the way to your own greatness.

My deeply-held intention is that this book provides you with the tools you need to begin to write a new story for yourself—a story full of gratitude and grace; a story that celebrates your beauty and world-changing gifts, and forgives your perceived imperfections.

Begin *now*. Tap into the power of the journaling prompts after each story. Read the book again from the beginning, and when you feel your higher self tapping you on the shoulder, imploring you to *pay attention* to a particular story or question, listen to that wisest part of you. If you do, you will receive gifts beyond imagining.

It is never too late to rewrite the stories of your past, and step into

245

a new, more vibrant truth. The authors in this book have paved the way; they are calling you to follow in their footsteps. All you need to do is set your feet on the path, and grace will walk beside you.

Love, and many blessings,

Bryna René Haynes
Chief Editor, Inspired Living Publishing

ABOUT OUR
Authors

Dr. Taura L. Barr, PhD, RN, FAHA, is an alum of the Robert Wood Johnson Foundation Nurse Faculty Scholars program, a holistic health advocate, and an internationally-recognized expert in the genomics of stroke. She is the founder of CereDx and Deep Roots Healing, and is passionate about incorporating intentional wellness in the care and recovery of stroke patients and creating a new model for treating brain injury: patient-centered integrative holistic healthcare, guided by patient-specific needs on a continuum. Learn more at **www.DeepRootsHealing.org** and download your free Integrative Health and Wellness Assessment™.

Diana Beaulieu is an intuitive coach, teacher, healer and storyteller and a passionate advocate for women who seek to live an authentic, sacred life. Diana has spent fifteen years on a mission to help women to heal and step onto their path of feminine power. She is the founder of Sacred Woman Awakening, a unique learning and healing program for women who wish to recover their Divine Feminine connection in a tangible and experiential way. Claim your free gift at **www.SacredWomanCoaching.com.**

Alex Bratty is a certified coach, professional speaker, and best-selling author. She works with female entrepreneurs to help them nail their niche, master their message, and put an effective marketing strategy in place so they can create a thriving business. With an MBA and almost twenty years of experience, Alex has worn multiple hats in business, from management level in a Fortune 500 company to partner in a multi-million-dollar firm to entrepreneur of a six-figure company. Connect with her at **www.AlexBratty.com.**

Sheila Callaham is a best-selling author and intuitive success coach with a passion for motivating women to chase their dreams with wild abandon. She founded The Authentic Author platform to encourage writers to move from wanna-be authors to gonna-be authors. Learn more at **www.SheilaCallaham.com** and claim your free gift, "Five Must-Dos Before You Write Your Book."

Jill Celeste, MA is a best-selling author, marketing teacher, and founder of the Celestial Marketing Academy, an online school for purpose-driven entrepreneurs who want to learn how to become the Director of Marketing for their businesses. Committed to offering affordable marketing instruction, Jill believes that entrepreneurs should not go into debt to get the marketing help they need. Visit **www.JillCeleste.com** to download a free copy of her book, *That First Client*, and other free resources.

Laura Clark, known as the Soul Wise Living Mentor, helps overwhelmed professionals stop listening to the negativity within them and get off the emotional rollercoaster that delays action. She uses a unique blend of spiritual awakening tools that teach you to hear their own intuition more consistently, understand it more clearly and act upon it more courageously. Her clients discover how to quickly lead the inspired life filled with joy and abundance that they so want. Discover more at **www.SoulWiseLiving.com** and download your Soul Wise Living Compass Guide.

Stacey Curnow is a purpose and success coach who recently left behind a twenty-year career in nurse-midwifery to help women (and some very cool men) give birth to their BIG dreams. She is the author of the critically-acclaimed children's book, *Ravenna*, and coauthor of two international best-selling books, including *Inspiration for a Woman's Soul: Choosing Happiness*. Learn more at **www.StaceyCurnow.com** and download your free gift, "The Purpose and Passion Guidebook."

Felicia D'Haiti is an Energy Empowerment and Feng Shui Coach and cancer survivor, who guides clients in shifting their perspectives and environments to move beyond perfectionism, fear, and self-imposed limitations. Felicia is a long-time educator, Interior Alignment® Feng Shui and Space Clearing Teacher and Reiki Master. She is a contributing author in *Inspiration for a Woman's Soul: Cultivating Joy* and several other books. She lives in Maryland with her husband and four children. Learn more at **www.FeliciaDHaiti.com** and download your "Get Clear on Your Space Starter Kit."

Through her own experiences of addiction, depression, and loss, **Mal Duane** has transformed her life and recreated herself as an awakened, authentic woman. Now, she helps women heal their broken hearts and reclaim their lives. A best-selling author, inspirational speaker, and coach, she has been featured on Fox News, CBS Radio, and over 200 internet radio shows, and is a contributor to MariaShriver. com, *Huffington Post, Healthy Living*, and *Aspire Magazine*. Reach Mal at **www. MalDuaneCoach.com.**

Bailey Frumen, MSW, LCSW, is a psychotherapist, writer, speaker, and transformational success coach. Through her Clarity Master Program, live events, and coaching, she helps ambitious women ditch fear and take action on living a life they love. She has been named "One of the Top 20 Life Coaches to Watch" by Popexpert.com. Her work has been published in *Huffington Post*, *Elephant Journal*, *Aspire Magazine*, *Natural Awakenings*, *Popexpert*, and numerous guest blogs. Learn more at **www.BaileyFrumen.com**.

Dr. Colleen Georges is a nationally-certified psychologist, certified Positive Psychology Coach, speaker, and best-selling author who helps her clients see all the good within and around them. Colleen blogs at *Seeing All The Good* and *Huffington Post*, and is a coauthor of *The Wisdom of Midlife Women 2*, *Unleash Your Inner Magnificence*, *Contagious Optimism*, *10 Habits of Truly Optimistic People*, *101 Great Ways to Enhance Your Career*, and *The Book of Success*. Learn more at **www. LifeCoachingNJ.com**.

Kelley Grimes, MSW, is a counselor, speaker, author, and self-nurturing expert. She is passionate about empowering overwhelmed and exhausted individuals to live with more peace, joy, and meaning through the practice of self-nurturing. Kelley also provides professional and leadership development to organizations dedicated to making the world a better place. She is married to an artist, has two empowered daughters, and loves singing with a small women's group. Learn more at **www. KelleyGrimes.com** and download your free "Self-Nurturing Mobile App."

Zinnia Gupte is an inspirational author, speaker, priestess and sacred dancer who helps women embrace their sacred feminine power. She is the best-selling author of *Messages From Shakti*, host of the Shakti Power podcast on iTunes, and a *Huffington Post* blogger. Zinnia leads empowerment workshops in New York and teaches sacred dance every year in Spain at the Ibiza Spirit Festival. Reach her at **www. ShaktiPriestess.com** and receive your complimentary Shakti Goddess Gift Bundle!

Pamela Henry is a certified Life Coach, best-selling author, inspirational writer, and singer-songwriter. She works with women who feel like their best years are behind them, and helps them to get clear on what they really want and finally make their dreams happen. Through her coaching and writing practices, Pamela helps her clients simplify the process of creating an extraordinary life—a life where they shine with confidence in everything they do. Learn more at **www.PamelaHenry.com**, and sign up for your free "5-day Jump-Start Your Extraordinary Life" mini-course.

Cindy Hively is the Founder and Goddess Creatrix for In Her Fullness. She empowers spiritual women to create an abundant life they love by stepping into their own unique Fullness Lifestyle. She helps them to remove blockages and strategize and optimize key areas of their lives to experience a luscious, Rhythmic life overflowing with love, greatest joys, vibrant health, personal success, practical lifestyle, sacred ritual, feminine mystery, spiritual connection, juicy fun and prosperity. Learn more at **www.InHerFullness.com** and sign up for your free gift, "The Sensuous Breath Meditation."

Stacey Hoffer is a self-love guide, feminine inner wisdom coach, blogger, author, and sacred circle holder. As the founder of Soul Alignment Living Mom Renewal Circles, Stacey works with women who are ready to choose self-love over fear, guilt, shame, and stress, and live in more alignment with their hearts and souls. Her message for women around the world is: Live your best life. Honor your body, mind, and spirit. Practice peace, love, and happiness. And trust your inner feminine wisdom. Learn more at **www.StaceyHoffer.com** and download your free "Soul Alignment Living Starter Kit."

Bev Janisch is a mindful living coach, speaker and author. Bev mentors women who are ready to take an inner journey to connect with themselves and gain clarity in order to live a life full of meaning and inner contentment. Bev empowers women with a proven mindfulness-based system of powerful tools and techniques to transform their lives from the inside out. Women who work with Bev are guaranteed to ignite their inner sparkle. Learn more and download your "Ignite Your Inner Sparkle Kit" at **www.TheCompassionateMind.ca/inner-sparkle-kit**.

Dr. Angela M. Joyner is the Founder of The Wonder Loft, a positive leadership coaching practice for women. Through her writing, teaching, and leading curated workshop experiences, Angela helps women discover their unique brilliance, have more confidence and flourish. Her mission is to nourish the minds and souls of women around the world. Learn more at **www.TheWonderLoft.com** and get your free "Have More Confidence" CD.

Shelley Lundquist is an international best-selling author, motivational speaker, and Self-Mastery & Success Coach who uses her intuitive gifts and transformational breakthrough processes to empower audiences all over the world in leveraging the unlimited power of their own potential. By guiding you through a journey of self-discovery and a shift in the way you perceive yourself and the world, Shelley will help you create your best life: a peaceful, harmonious life of joy and abundance that acknowledges body, mind, and spirit. Learn more and claim your free gift at **www. ShelleyLundquist.com.**

Beth Marshall is a transformational trainer, coach, author, and speaker who is inspired to serve self-motivated and high-energy professionals and entrepreneurs to heal and transform their relationships with money to maximize the amount of freedom, choice, and peace that they have in their lives. As a CPA, an MBA, and a Spiritual Financial Mentor, Beth offers a uniquely-blended practical and spiritual approach to finances that is action-oriented, non-judgmental, and compassionate. Learn more at **www.FinanciallyAuthentic.com,** and download your free copy of "3 Steps to Design Your Financial Plan, Save Money, and Get Out of Debt."

Sought-after Relationship Expert ***Stacey Martino*** and her husband Paul Martino empower individuals with the tools & strategies to transform their relationships. You do not need your partner to participate for this to work for you! Thousands of people have transformed their relationships using their proven programs and live events! The Martinos are the founders of **www.RelationshipDevelopment.org** and creators of RelationshipU®! Download their free e-book "It Does Not Take Two to Tango: How One Partner Can Transform Any Relationship in 8 Simple Steps" at **www.RelationshipTransformationSystem.com/freebook.**

Dr. Kimberly McGeorge, ND, CNH, is an Energy Frequency Expert, Naturopathic Doctor, and Certified Nutritional Herbologist. Dr. Kimberly teaches "quantum physics with a twist." She has over twenty-six years of clinical experience in alternative health and energy healing, and has worked on tens of thousands of clients in clinical practice and remotely. Kimberly is able to remove blocks and rebalance energy in any area of your life. Learn more at **www.KimberlyMcGeorge.com.**

Tonya Melendez is an International Psychic Medium, TV & radio personality, Spiritual Leadership Coach and mentor, creator of the Virtual Psychic Summit, writer, and blogger for *Huffington Post*. Listening to Spirit as an intimate connection to your spirit, Tonya radiates love and positive energy, thus guiding you to a better understanding of yourself and your life with grace and gratitude. The gift of intuitive insight creates opportunities for her to guide and heal people around the world. #ServeShareShine is her mantra; she is currently, loving, living and learning in Mexico. Find her at **www.TarotLifeCoach.com.**

Suzanne Moore helps coaches and consultants create success by teaching them how to build their e-mail marketing list. Her no-nonsense straight talk, clear direction, and technical know-how provide the support her clients need to "get out of their own way" and get clients. Suzanne has an MBA, is a member of the Change Your Attitude … Change Your Life Good Life Team, and is a featured expert on New York's WOR radio station. Learn more at **www.SuzanneTMoore.com** and download your free gift, "40 Ways to Build Your E-mail List."

Stacey Murphy is the Queen of Juicy Love, a best-selling author, and founder of the Blissful Lotus School of Loving Arts. Through her private coaching and group programs, she teaches women how to love themselves, attract their ideal relationships, and master erotic skills to blow his mind. Using the Tantric philosophy of seduction, Stacey teaches couples how to effectively seduce each other in the 4 Pillars of Love: mental, emotional, physical and sexual. Download your free gift, "The Love Mojo Reboot 30-Day Program," at **https://TheBlissfulLotus.leadpages. co/love-mojo-reboot-kit.**

Peggy Nolan is the host of the popular podcast, *Let Go Move Forward*, and coauthor of four best-selling books. Peggy is passionate about leadership and personal growth. She teaches yoga, she's a third-level black prajioud in Muay Thai Kickboxing, and she's a breast cancer survivor who's been slaying doubt and vanquishing fear since 2004. Peggy lives in Derry, NH with her husband, Richard. Connect with Peggy at **www.PeggyNolan.com.**

Dr. Bonnie Nussbaum, PhD, psychologist and holistic coach, believes we are capable of far more than we think. She owns Empowerment Coaching, LLC and a mom-n-pop motel that she's rehabbing into a retreat center with Native American structures and a labyrinth. Bonnie draws on intuitive guidance from her spiritual team, along with holistic tools and humor for empowering clients to soar to their full potential. Download "Ten Minutes to Breathing Life Into Your Life" at **www. EmpowermentAndPurpose.com.**

Dr. Mary E. Pritchard, PhD, HHC is an international bestselling author, esteemed blogger at *Psychology Today* and *Huffington Post*, and the Expert Body Love Columnist for *Aspire Magazine*. Dr. Mary is passionately dedicated to empowering today's women in healing their relationships with food, their bodies, and themselves, reconnecting with their Inner Goddess, and embracing the truth of who they are. Learn more at **www.DrMaryPritchard.com** and download your free 4-part self-love audio series and bonus worksheets.

Melissa Rapoport is a Food Relationship Expert. She works with people around the world who want to fit into their jeans, break the chains of emotional eating, say "No" to yo-yo dieting, and say "Yes" to food freedom, more energy, and increased happiness. She is also an international best-selling author. What makes Melissa different? She combines her graduate work in Developmental Psychology with her education in health and coaching to create programs the result in lifetime change. Find her at **www.MelissaRapoport.com.**

Lore Raymond (Lore rhymes with "story") founded Women as Visionaries and the Divine Dialogue Writing System™. A Peruvian shaman bestowed the title of *chacaruna*—a bridge person—upon her, which challenged her to help connect people to their authentic power and messages. She enjoys serving as a heart-centered visionary, spiritual tour guide, and transformational author, and leads women's Vision Quests. Learn more at **www.LoreRaymond.com** and download your free gift, "5 Journal Adventures to Recharge Your Creativity."

Consciously merging her practical tools as a psychologist with her intuitive and spiritual gifts, **Dr. Debra L. Reble** empowers women to connect with their hearts and live authentically through her transformational Soul-Hearted Living™ program. Debra is the author of the best-selling book *Being Love: How Loving Ourselves Creates Ripples of Transformation In Our Relationships and The World* (May 2016) and has coauthored two of ILP's best-selling collaborative books. She lives in Cleveland, OH with her soul partner, Doug, and her dog, Shiloh. Learn more at **www.DebraReble.com.**

Intuitive **Lisa Marie Rosati** is a leading Success and Business Coach for spiritual women and soulful entrepreneurs. She's the Creatrix of The Goddess Lifestyle Plan™, an expert columnist for *Aspire Magazine,* international best-selling author, and High Priestess of The Goddess Lifestyle Sisterhood™. Lisa has successfully built a thriving, global lifestyle business while raising her three children. It is her passion and divine purpose to inspire and teach women how to magically create an abundant, purposeful life and prosperous business they love. Download your free gift at **www.GoddessLifestylePlan.com.**

Shelley Riutta, MSE, LPC is the founder and President of the Global Association of Holistic Psychotherapy and Coaching, a Holistic Psychotherapist, and the creator of a 6-figure Holistic Psychotherapy practice. Because of her success at creating a thriving Holistic Practice, she launched the Global Association of Holistic Psychotherapy and Coaching (GAHP), which supports Holistic Therapists, Healers, Coaches, and Health Practitioners to develop Thriving 6-Figure Holistic Practices and learn about Holistic Methods™ to accelerate the results of their clients. Visit **www. TheGAHP.com** to claim your free gift.

A skilled, multi-tasking mother of four, Registered Nurse, and international best-selling author, **Kellyann Schaefer** is the CEO and Founder of Task Complete, a personal assistance and concierge service company. In business today, she upholds a mission of giving families and busy professionals reliable and compassionate assistance so they can focus their time on living a joyful, abundant life. She is also the creator of The Concierge Academy, where startup concierges learn how to become profitable industry leaders. To learn more, visit **www.TaskComplete.com** and download your free gift, "The Secrets to Doing Less and Living More."

Karen Smith is a woman on a mission to help you discover your purpose. She dares you to be bold, curious, take risks, have faith, and see through eyes of hope, easily accessing your higher wisdom! Her personal belief is that we all have the unlimited ability to create miracles and that each of us can dig beneath the layers that block our connection to love, unleashing the truth of who we are. She is the creator of the Purpose Formula, a unique system of using our brain-heart connection with managing the body's energy to unlock the life, love, and leadership we can fully live each day. Discover your purpose at **www.FindingPurpose.com**

Karen Spaiches is a personal life coach who engages with women who feel lost and unsettled. She helps clients unleash long-forgotten dreams, stop settling for the "good enough," and take passionate action in creating their ideal life! She nurtures and empowers women to live their highest potential through creating powerful habits of self-love and self-acceptance. Karen's personal rediscovery journey set the stage for her signature program, "Dream Life Design." Learn more at **www. KarenSpaiches.com.**

Sara Turner is an experienced Flower Essence Trainer and the Nature Kingdom Guide in her companies, Essentially Flowers and Create a Magical Business. Sara's passion is helping women experience the magic of their true potential and live meaningful, authentic lives with nature as their guide. Sara helps coaches and therapists merge the Divine Feminine energies of nature with practical skills to create magical lives and businesses. Visit **www.CreateAMagicalBusiness.com** and download your free report, "The Healer's Guide to Business Bliss."

Kailean Welsh, MS, LPC, is a Holistic Psychotherapist, Wisdom Teacher, and author. Specializing in practical spirituality, she is passionate about returning psychotherapy to its roots as "care of the soul." Kailean works with clients at her office in Wisconsin as well as virtually, offering transformational programs, presentations, and classes. With compassion and connection, she helps people heal at their core and "illuminate their best self." An avid reader, Kailean loves sunshine, water, biking, and family. Learn more at **www.KaileanWelsh.com** and download your free gift: "Five Spiritual Truths to Transform Your Life Now."

ABOUT THE
Publisher
Linda Joy

*F*ounded in 2010 by Inspirational Catalyst, Radio Show Host, and *Aspire Magazine* Publisher Linda Joy, Inspired Living Publishing (ILP) is an international best-selling inspirational boutique publishing company dedicated to spreading a message of love, positivity, feminine wisdom, and self-empowerment to women of all ages, backgrounds, and life paths. Linda's family of multimedia brands reach over 44,000 subscribers and a social media community of over 24,000 women.

Through our highly successful anthology division, we have brought six books and over 180 visionary female authors to best-seller status. Our powerful, high-visibility publishing, marketing, and list-building packages have brought these authors—all visionary entrepreneurs, coaches, therapists and health practitioners—the positive, dynamic exposure they need to attract their ideal audience and thrive in their businesses.

Inspired Living Publishing also publishes single-author books by visionary female authors whose messages are aligned with Linda's philosophy of authenticity, empowerment, and personal transformation. Recent best-selling releases include *Being Love: How Loving Yourself Creates Ripples of Transformation in Your Relationships and the World,* by Dr. Debra L. Reble; and *The Art of Inspiration: An Editor's Guide to Writing Powerful, Effective Inspirational & Personal Development Books,* by ILP Chief Editor Bryna René Haynes.

ILP's family of authors reap the benefits of being a part of a sacred family of inspirational multimedia brands which deliver the best in transformational and empowering content across a wide range of platforms. Our hybrid publishing packages and *à la carte*

255

marketing and media packages provide visionary female authors with access to our proven best-seller model and high-profile multimedia exposure across all of Linda's imprints (including *Aspire Magazine*, the "Inspired Conversations" radio show on OM Times Radio, the Inspired Living Giveaway, Inspired Living Secrets, and exposure to Linda's loyal personal audience of over 44,000 women and 24,000 social media followers).

If you're ready to publish your transformational book or share your sacred story in one of ours, we invite you to join us! Learn more about our publishing services at **www.InspiredLivingPublishing.com.**

Inspired Living Publishing ~ Transforming Women's Lives, One Story at a Time™

If you enjoyed this book, visit
www.InspiredLivingPublishing.com
and sign up for ILP's e-zine to receive news about hot new releases, promotions, and information on exciting author events.

ABOUT THE
Editor

Bryna René Haynes

"**W**ord Alchemist" Bryna René Haynes is the founder of The Heart of Writing, the chief editor for Inspired Living Publishing, and the best-selling author of *The Art of Inspiration: An Editor's Guide to Creating Powerful, Effective Inspirational and Personal Development Books* (2016). Her heart-centered editing and creation coaching services are designed to help inspired writers move through their blocks and perceived limitations, connect with their authentic voices, and create world-changing written works which transform their lives and businesses.

Bryna's editing portfolio includes numerous successful and best-selling non-fiction titles, including the four previous best-selling Inspired Living Publishing print anthologies: *Inspiration for a Woman's Soul: Cultivating Joy* (2015), *Inspiration for a Woman's Soul: Choosing Happiness* (2015), and *Embracing Your Authentic Self (2011),* and *A Juicy, Joyful Life* (2010).

Through her company, The Heart of Writing, Bryna and her team offer education, creative support, and professional editing services for authors, business owners, and bloggers in all genres.

Bryna lives outside of Providence, Rhode Island with her husband, Matthew, and their daughter, Áine. When she's not writing, you can find her teaching yoga philosophy, practicing her landscape photography, and singing with her little Moonbeam.

Learn more about Bryna, meet The Heart of Writing Team, and download your free 45-page e-book, *The 5 Secrets of Powerful Writing,* at **www.TheHeartofWriting.com.**

257

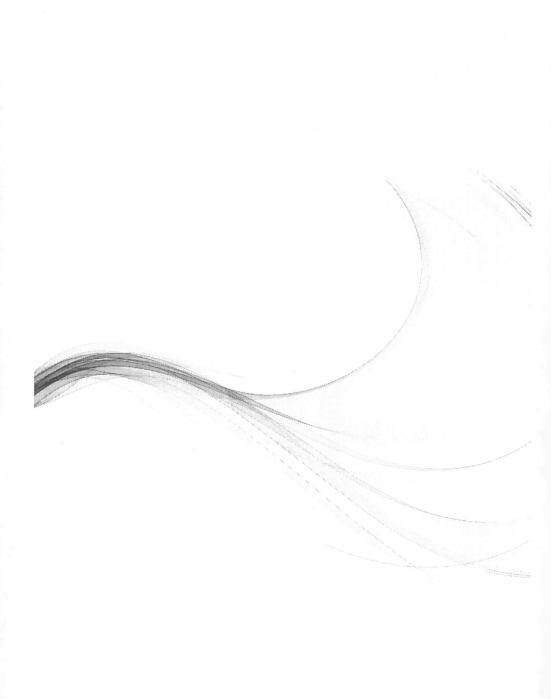